Wake-Up Call
A Mother's Grief Journey

**THE CALL THAT CHANGES YOUR LIFE
FOREVER**

Cherie Rickard RN, CGC

Editor
Todd Horne

AVAILABLE ON EBOOK

Cherie Rickard/Cherie Rickard Enterprises

Maurepas, LA/70449

www.Cherierickard.com

Email: info@cherierickard.com

Book Layout ©2017 JF Book Designs

Ordering Information:

Quantity sales. Special discounts are available on quantity purchases by corporations, associations, and others. For details, contact the "Special Sales Department" at the email address above.

Wake-Up Call...A Mother's Grief Journey/ Cherie Rickard. —1st ed.

ISBN 978-1503129122

Contents

FORWARD

In my many years of ministry as a pastor and a Deputy/Chaplain with a local Sheriff's Department, I have seen more than my share of families suffering with sudden tragedy and loss. I met Cherie Rickard not long after she had said her final farewell to her son Bryant. I was so amazed at the strength and tenacity she displayed while processing her grief. Cherie is an extraordinary woman and my life is richer for having known her.

In her book, "Wake up Call," Cherie is painfully honest in her description of how to deal with grief God's way. Her book is not an "impersonal" or "clinical" step by step manual of how to deal with the stages of grief. Instead, it is refreshingly thoughtful and an honest look into how a Christian parent can grieve with hope after losing a child.

Cherie proves that God will never waste our pain and can give you true Beauty for Ashes.

Dy. Ken Spivey

Ascension Parish Sheriff's Office Chaplain

"The Last Enemy to be destroyed is death."

- 1 CORINTHIANS 15:26

"If we are in a battle with this enemy called Death, I believe we should learn about it, in order to know how to confront the dying experience.

We need to know how to face that enemy on our own behalf, and how to deal with the inevitable deaths of loved ones and friends. The last enemy that will be abolished is death."

- Billy Graham, 'Death and the Life After'

CHAPTER 1

A Glimpse

T he first time I saw my baby boy Bryant in the hospital delivery room on a late summer afternoon in a Montgomery, Alabama hospital after just having given birth to him, I knew without question he was a special gift from God. To me, and I am certain to me alone, at that moment, there was something almost divine about him.

Laying eyes on him for that very first time, I cannot even begin to explain the swell of love and absolute connection that surged inside of me. I not only felt overwhelmingly blessed, but I was convinced this precious baby boy was a gift from God to me. I also knew in my heart this gift would last a lifetime. Bryant was my second child, but my first son, and I could not help myself. I marveled in amazement at how beautiful he was, yes, even in those first few seconds. Bryant Carlton Kite, with those piercing dark eyes and smooth olive skin, was certainly all boy and was beautiful.

Everyone else there that day thought so, too. And Bryant was also large. He weighed in at 9 pounds. I remember thinking right off the bat that one day he was going to be an athlete of some kind. I could just feel it. He had that look athletes have, even as a newborn. It's that look you just can't describe when you are in their presence. But you know. somehow, you just know. I knew Bryant was special the first few seconds I met him. But there was so much I didn't know.

It was June 5, 1990. I was 24- years-old – practically a baby still myself in many ways -- and, of course, I naturally wanted nothing more in all the world than to hold my son in my arms. The nurses, though, would not let me. I had barely touched his beautiful little face when the nurses betrayed me and hurriedly whisked Bryant away without an explanation. Shocked and unsure of what was happening, I felt a tremor in my heart. I remember a strange, uneasy feeling overwhelmed me instantly. It was the same feeling all mothers succumb to when we know something is just not right. I've been a nurse for most of my professional life, but on that day I had not yet started nursing school.

When I recall those first moments of Bryant's life, I realize how much of a blessing it was that I hadn't begun my training yet because if I knew then what I now know, I would have leapt off of that delivery table that day and chased down those Judases who were taking my baby away from me. I would have wreaked havoc and created chaos all in an effort to save Bryant's life. As it was, I had no idea what was wrong, if anything. I had no idea what was going on. All I knew for sure was I wanted to hold my beautiful baby and for him to be beside me, in my presence. From that very first moment, I wanted Bryant with me. I wanted to hold him – forever. But, before that could even happen, I realized how precious little control I had. God obviously had other plans. We always want to know everything, to be in control of our lives, to supervise and manage situations, especially as mothers to our children. It's instinctual and in our blood. I believe with all my heart that God has infused this into our natures as mothers.

But God, I also believe, knows everything. At that moment on that particular day, God knew what I didn't know and He had it planned that way. The next few hours would be the most trying of my life up to the point. They brought me to my knees, literally.

CHAPTER 2

❋

Bryant's Struggle Breaks Me

B
ryant's life was in jeopardy, the doctor explained to me a few hours later. The thought of losing him broke me completely. I went from feeling like something wasn't right to knowing there were serious problems later that evening when my pediatrician came in and explained the dire situation my baby faced.

Bryant's birth was a planned C-section. My doctor told me that when they pulled Bryant from my womb he had opened his mouth. Bryant swallowed and aspirated a great deal of fluid. He was experiencing serious respiratory stress. My baby was struggling to breath. He might make it. Might.

The doctor told me Bryant had a 50/50 chance of pulling through. She also said his size could help him, but we would have to wait and see.

She then told me Bryant's left ureter had a small obstruction. After he made it through the respiratory distress and was breathing well enough on his own, she explained Bryant would need further testing on his ureter. The doctor left me by myself. I was alone in my hospital room worried about Bryant. Surely, I had done something wrong. There had to be something I could have done differently during the pregnancy, while planning the C-section, I thought. What had I done? What could I do now? Bryant's fighting to stay alive in another room where I can't see him or be with him, and I am all alone in the hospital powerless with nowhere to turn. Mindlessly flipping channels on the TV in my room, I landed on a local Christian channel. They were about to go off the air, taking last-minute prayer requests. I reached for the phone and started punching in the numbers flashing on the TV screen. The program was ending; no way am I going to get through. But I kept punching.

That's when it happened. I'll never forget it. I heard a voice ask me, "Do you? Do you have any prayer requests?"

"Yes!"

"Yes, I do."

With every ounce of energy, I had in me I tried to speak without crying, but I just couldn't do it. "My son was just born and they tell me he has a 50/50 chance of pulling through his respiratory distress without pneumonia setting in and possibly causing him to die. Can you pray for him?" By now, the ending credits had started rolling on the TV screen before me. This show was over. Through the rolling credits in the background I saw someone wearing a headset and handing a piece of paper to the pastors. It was a lady and a man he gave the note to, and they literally said, "We have a prayer request that is too important to pass, let's hold on just a minute," the lady pastor said. Time was stopping.

"There is a young lady in the hospital that needs prayer for her newborn son. She has been told he may not make it and we need to lift up this child in prayer; need to lift this mother up in prayer." In the midst of my deep sadness, worry, guilt and utter broken- ness, they prayed for me and with me. The feelings of loneliness and despair turned to hope and security. I felt like I had a thousand angels watching over me at that very moment. I felt God. I knew God was real. In that instant, I knew He was real, and I knew that no matter what anyone said Bryant was going to live, and Bryant was going to be fine.

Broken and completely dependent, I turned to God. He came to me alone in my hospital room when I didn't know Him. He called to me and I reached for Him and shared my heart with Him. I submitted to him transparently and without holding anything back. I did this publicly, where anyone watching and paying attention could see. I said, "Yes" and "I do" to my God. At that moment, that very moment, I gained knowledge of God personally that I never knew before. Unflinchingly, God reassured me. He gave me strength, courage, and peace. From God, through God and to God, I had faith. A gift.

Bryant was alive and he would live, forever, I believed. I thought when I first met him that Bryant was a gift that would last a lifetime. I was so grateful to know this now. My idea of a lifetime and God's knowledge of one, however, still didn't quite align. But, through His grace, He had given me Bryant to demonstrate this to me. Of course, I wasn't aware of that then. All I knew was my baby was going to live.

Five days later I was discharged from the hospital. Bryant had to remain a while longer. And I had to explain to a very loving 2-year-old big sister, Kristina, why her baby brother wasn't with me when I came home.

CHAPTER 3

Looking Back

"In his heart a man plans his course, but the LORD determines his steps."

- Proverbs 16:9

When I look back on Bryant's first day on Earth and when I look back on his entire life, I can see the hand of God working in his life, my life and the lives of my family and the lives of all of the people Bryant came in contact with during his 17 years here. It was St. Augustine who said that if people had a choice of either dying or reliving their lives over again, they would most certainly choose death because of all the danger and evil they so narrowly escaped. I understand the sentiment in that statement, but I believe in my heart God has determined and that we are destined to choose life every step of the way, first in this part of our life on Earth, and then whenever God determines for us in Heaven, eternally. We don't have the wisdom, the strength, the courage, the stamina or the required inspiration to live independent of God, though. God created us to look to Him for life.

Bryant showed me that about God. Looking back, we can see how much we have accomplished and suffered without even trying or thinking about it, even against our wishes and wills. So often, we give such little thought to what we are doing before it occurs – often times even when it is happening. Looking back, after everything has been carried out, we are amazed and we say, "Why did these things happen to me when I never thought about them or when I thought something completely different would happen?" Clearly, Proverbs 16:9 is true: "In his heart a man plans his course, but the LORD determines his steps," even against our plans and wills. In my understandings, we have no choice when faced with Truth but to agree that our own cleverness and foresight don't guide our lives and actions. God's wonderful power, wisdom, and good ness not only guide us, He carries us.

Only as we look back do we fully recognize how often God was with us when we neither saw his hand nor felt his presence at the time it was happening. Peter said, "He cares for you." (1 Peter 5:7). Looking back on Bryant's time here, it's obvious to me our own lives would prove that God tenderly carries us in his arms. When we look back on how God has led and brought us through so much evil, adversity and danger, we can clearly see the ever present goodness of God.

His thoughts and His ways are so far above our thoughts, minds, and perception.

CHAPTER 4

❋

Extended Stay

L eaving Bryant at the hospital once I was discharged was very hard – for me and also for his big sister. I wanted to breast feed Bryant, so I would go to the hospital any and every time they would allow me to and try to feed him.

It was a very trying and desperate feeling. Kristina, bless her precious heart, simply could not understand why we had to leave "our baby" at the hospital and not just bring him home to be with us. I tried to explain it to her the best I could, but that didn't really work out too well.

Ten days later, I was able to walk right out of that hospital with my new baby and Kristina was so excited. Kristina and Bryant grew up together very close. Yes, through the years, they fought like all siblings do, but they loved each other more than any two kids I have ever seen. Three months after bringing Bryant home, we were back in the care of the doctors with him, this time in Birmingham. I took him to the children's hospital to check on his ureter obstruction discovered at birth. They told me that the obstruction was small and not very likely to cause him any problems. Contact sports while growing up would not be best, they advised, but to have him checked him again in a few months and then again later on while he was going through puberty because of the strain the kidneys have during that time of a child's life.

They were right.

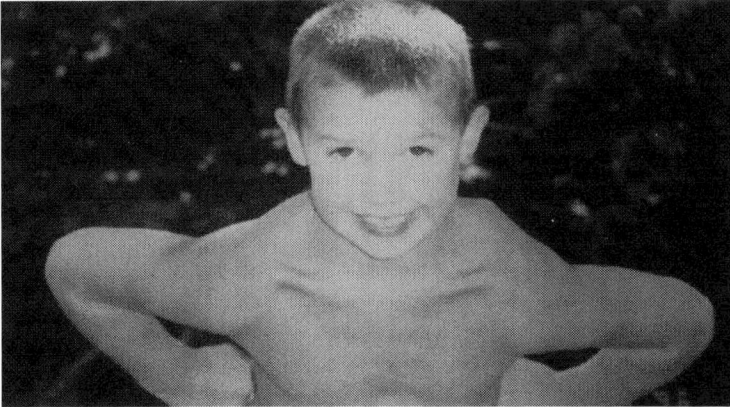

Bryant lived a very healthy life and never really had any issues from the obstruction. He had typical allergies; some skin dermatitis irritations, though he never complained. Bryant rarely complained about anything his whole life. Every once in a while you would see him itching and rubbing lotion on his skin. That's the only way I ever really knew when his dermatitis was flaring up. Bryant grew up playing sports. He made great grades in school, and he always made really good friends. I can honestly say there was never a teacher that didn't adore my Bryant. He was the cutest little boy, always getting bumps and bruises along the way, loving baseball more than any other sport. He tried football against my better judgment, but, as parents, we do what we can to please our babies. Bryant was barely 8 when his father and I first separated then soon after divorced. When you get to the point of truly believing your children would be better off if you and your husband were apart, then it's way past due time to make a change. I don't believe anyone ever sets out planning divorce when they are married. The painful truth is that we all, at one time or another, have thought while married we would rather be alone than in our current life situation. You can't control or change someone else so you have to do what's best for you and your children.

Divorce is painful and confusing for everyone, even the person that initiates the separation. I initiated our separation and divorce because I saw no other way for my kids or for myself. The scary fact is one out of every two marriages will end in divorce and most of these marriages have children. It's difficult but I know I tried really hard to remember while I was caught up in my own problems that I was still most important to my kids. Parents always are most important to their children even if the children don't always say it, even they aren't consciously aware of your importance to their lives.

While you may feel either devastated, or even relieved, your divorce leaves your children frightened and confused by the loss of security in their life. More than ever, you have to give your child all of the love, support, and guidance he or she needs, even though everything seems much more difficult and more complicated. All children handle divorce in different ways at different ages.

I think Bryant actually handled our divorce easier than my daughter who was 10 when we separated. We were at each other's throats and both believed we were right and the other person wrong in virtually every conversation. It seemed to become almost impossible to build a co-parenting relationship. I did not seek therapy for my children and whether that was the right or wrong decision to make, who knows? Who really knows when you or your child should see a therapist? You have to know your child and know what age-appropriate discussions should be for addressing sensitive issues.

Probably the biggest challenge I faced as the divorce process wore on was how to navigate the emotional turmoil of custody and visitation when I clearly believed I, as their mother, was the perfect caregiver for my children. Bryant would just go with the flow. He did not want to upset either of us, which was painfully obvious to me. I found myself having to just relinquish my desires and opinions so as not to upset my children, and believe me; I didn't do that with ease.

In order to stop the fighting sometimes you have to just do it yourself. Watching your son feel like he needs to protect you at the age of 8 is not natural or right in any circumstance. I don't ever believe Bryant or Kristina felt they were responsible for our divorce as some children do but I also never felt Bryant wanted his father and me together and he was noticeably happier when his dad and I were apart, or at least he did when he was with me. You only want to help your child deal with this change in their life so that they can cope with fears about separation. Bryant had to endure it all from separation to divorce and also the introducing of a significant other into the family, to ultimately learning to cope and be happy with a new step-family.

I recall finally realizing my children and I had conquered it all and really never missed a beat, celebrating holidays, birthday parties as I had always planned and shopping for back to school and Easter clothes all as we had always done, but then the hardest decision of all was what to do about moving away. I wanted to just pick up and go. I needed to establish residency for Kristina and Bryant and I had always known I would move back home to Louisiana one day.

But when you're divorced nothing ever works out exactly as you want it to because when you have children you always have their father to consider. Whether ex-spouses are in your life or not, they actually always are. We actually all discussed our plans to move as a family with Bryant's dad and his wife at the time that he had recently married. It seemed to be a good plan, and with my ability to travel and work in both Louisiana and Tennessee it was ideal for everyone at the time. I tried to sell Bryant on moving believe me, I tried. But he just wouldn't budge. He said, "Mom, just let me graduate with my friends and I will go to college and spend the rest of my life with you." I even introduced him to the baseball coach at the local high school in Louisiana where we had moved, and as impressed as Bryant admitted he was with the team and the school, he couldn't leave his close friends and teammates at Cordova High.

I respected my kids and their decisions as long as they were not too ridiculous. Bryant always had a good head on his shoulders and his convincing charm and beautiful smile was simply more than I could deny. Of course there were issues of holidays, money and curfews that my ex-husband and I argued over but if we could have agreed on everything to begin with we would not have ended up divorced.

Wendell was always so protective and as a step- dad (we never used that term, really), Bryant and Kristina loved Wendell very much the whole time they were growing up. When Wendell and I had Carson, well, that just brought us all together as a family, along with Wendell's daughter who didn't live with us but came to visit us as often as she could. The kids got along great. Kristina was always the mother figure to them and Bryant was the one who played up to her and was very laid back, helped with anything you asked, and was always very respectful of adults. He loved kids; he would play games with Carson and watch cartoons with him just to spend time with him.

WENDELL and BRYANT

I met my husband only four months after Bryant's dad and I separated. Very causally, I introduced him to Bryant and Kristina, but only after I felt this man was my soul mate. Wendell met Bryant when Bryant was almost 9 and Wendell even attended Bryant's birthday party and picked out his wrestler birthday cake that year. Bryant was a quiet, content child and never had a lot to say. He was always so very comfortable around Wendell. Wendell's daughter Mackenzie was only three-years old and Bryant was so sweet to her. They skated together at Bryant's birthday party. I can still see that it my mind right now so clearly, it was so cute.

I married Wendell on September 3, 1999 and was pregnant with Carson in December. Kristina and Bryant were so excited, Bryant always wanted to listen to my stomach to see if he could hear him and he anxiously asked every week, "When is he going to come out?" That made for a very long nine months. When Carson was born it was love at first sight for both of my kids. Bryant was protective and proud. We packed up and went to all of Bryant's baseball games and Carson grew up with a love of sports just like his brother and Dad.

Bryant and Carson, although 10 years apart, were very close and loved each other so much. Carson's hero was his big brother in every sense of the word. Wendell was so great to my kids and I had a life that a woman could only dream of.

This is the life I always wanted to have, beautiful children to watch grow and a loving husband side-by-side with me.

Of course, looking back, Bryant seemed to grow up and mature so fast.

When he turned 16, Bryant wanted a truck so badly. He deserved one, too. So, a month after his 16th birthday, Wendell took Bryant to pick out a truck. He was so excited. I, however, was so nervous about him driving, but I knew I had to get him his own vehicle. His Dad moved a few miles away from Bryant's high school in Tennessee and I had just completed the move back to Louisiana in order to establish residency for Kristina, who would be attending LSU soon. I made the decision to move to Louisiana while Kristina and Bryant were still in high school in Tennessee with the best intentions in mind for my whole family.

My daughter always wanted to go to LSU, ever since she was a little girl. She always had LSU memorabilia as a child –clothes, stuffed Mike the Tigers, and blankets. She was born in Baton Rouge and later, after moving to Memphis, she clearly always kept that root connection to home. Because I knew she was an LSU Tiger at heart, I knew I needed to establish residency for her in some way. It was an extremely tough decision, but I knew in the long run my moving to Louisiana and leaving two of my babies in Memphis would be for the best.

Carson, my youngest little boy, was four-years- old and it was important that we move before he started Kindergarten at a new school. Of course, I can still remember that move, too.

CHAPTER 5

✵

Life Transitions

December 26, 2004. Freezing in Memphis that day. Roads iced over everywhere, the interstate a slate of snow and ice mixed together. We actually had to shovel the drive way and walkways just to move things from the house to the moving van using a dolly. Bryant was going with us to Louisiana in the moving caravan to help us move and to spend the rest of Christmas break with us. We had just found a new lot we liked and we would start building in a week.

We needed to move almost all of our belongings into storage and then stay with my sister until our house was built. I had planned the years to come in my mind carefully. I knew I could go to Memphis every other week and work. I was a nurse, and working through an agency helped me work out my plan. For five days, I would work in Memphis, spending as much time as I could between 12-hour shifts with Kristina and Bryant.

They were both in school all day, so I could drive to the baseball field and sit in my car and watch practice before driving to work the 12- hour night shift. On my off days, I would spend them waiting for

Bryant and Kristina to be available for dinner. I would drive back to Louisiana PRN (the as needed shift) at the local hospital, spend as much time with my husband and my youngest son as possible, then turn back around and drive back to Memphis. Then, I would start all over again. This may seem hectic – and it was but I knew it would pay off later when Kristina would enroll at LSU.

Bryant would follow his sister to Tiger land soon after. That was the plan.

Bryant was a wonderful athlete, a great baseball player, and I wanted him to go to a college that had an awesome baseball team. So, what better team than LSU, right?

For 18 months I drove back and forth, literally living in my friend Pam's house and taking over her daughter Ashton's bedroom. Ashton made jokes about it and, over time, began to call her room my room. Bryant was a good driver, and since he made really good grades, and since he needed a way to and from school every day, it seemed like a great idea to buy him a truck. In July 2006, my husband Wendell and Bryant went truck shopping. Bryant found the truck he wanted and, of course, Wendell found one, too.

Wendell bought Bryant a truck and he bought one for himself, too. They were two happy guys! Bryant couldn't wait to get the accessories for his new truck that Wendell had agreed to buy for him.

Bryant was always so appreciative for everything people did for him and for the things he was given. Back and forth from Louisiana to Memphis Bryant would drive his truck and, like I said, he was a really good driver. Bryant always wore this strap around his neck after he got his truck. His keys dangled from it. I never knew why he wore the strap – was it because he didn't like them in his pocket, or was it because he wanted the world to know he owned a truck? Whatever the reason, Bryant wore those keys everywhere. By December, he wanted to take Wendell up on that first accessory purchase. Bryant wanted pipes for his truck. He not only wanted you to see him coming down the street he wanted to hear him coming, too. Of course, he got those pipes put on his truck that Christmas in Louisiana and he could not wait to drive back to Memphis and show them off to all of his friends. He was so cute about the pipes, too. When we got home after having the pipes installed that day, Bryant sat in the driveway and wanted me to stand there while he turned his truck off and on over and over again just so I could hear the truck start up with the new pipes roaring and grumbling. It made him smile. I always felt good when I made Bryant smile. Bryant's smile is like a shining star you see it when everything else is dark around you. He always had a way of lighting of a room with his smile, his laugh and his jokes. I loved listening to the music he makes when he plays his guitar, also.

"Come in here, Mom, and listen to this," Bryant would say. He perfected "Sweet Home Alabama" and he would play that over and over for me. Since he was born in Alabama that particular song was very important for him to learn to play. He did. Bryant's the kind of son that makes you want to get up and cook a big breakfast just because you know he wants to eat; the kind of teenager that makes a mistake and learns from it, then turns around and teaches others to learn from it, too.

Bryant never wanted anyone mad at anyone. "Just blow it off," he would say. "Don't worry about that," or "Just relax!" I can still hear him saying that today. I don't even have to close my eyes to hear his voice. His friends nicknamed "Be Easy" because of his penchant for not letting things bother him and for encouraging others to follow that example.

So, there we were with Bryant still in Memphis living with his Dad, my husband, my youngest son and me living in Louisiana and my daughter in the dorms at LSU. Life was hectic, but good. Really good, as a matter of fact.

I would think all of the time about how much better it would be when we were all living in the same location again – my kids through college and settled down with their spouses and my grandchildren all living right here.

Sometimes our plans are not God's plans and we have to wait on Him. Waiting on God is a part of an unceasing prayer life. To wait is not merely to remain impassive. It is to expect -- to look for with patience, and also with submission. It is to long for, but not impatiently; to look for, but not to fret at the delay; to watch for, but not restlessly; to feel that if He does not come we will acquiesce, and yet to refuse to let the mind acquiesce in the feeling that He will not come.

ALL-STAR HIGH SCHOOL 1ST BASEMEN WITH LSU DREAMS

CHAPTER 6

✳

Curve Balls, Sinkers & Accessories

In January 2007, my daughter decided she needed to be with her friends from highs school and decided to leave LSU and move to Knoxville to attend the University of Tennessee. To say I was upset would be an understatement. But I had to let her go, as much as I wanted her here with me, and at LSU, I had come to the realization that we can only pave the way for our children, the path they choose is ultimately up to them.

I knew with one more year of high school left for Bryant he would come here and go to college at LSU. We talked about it all the time. I use to tell him how cute he was going to be in those purple and gold baseball uniforms. We all continued to live in different places but somehow made it work and we still managed to spend good quality time together. Bryant would drive to Louisiana every chance he could, I would drive to Memphis every month and Kristina would fly down to Louisiana and visit every 6-8 weeks. I see now, when I think back on it, how we were able to spend quality time because of our limited time.

I personally knew mothers who had teenagers living in their own homes and yet they still never saw or spent much time with them. When both parents are working and kids going to school and playing sports, the time we have together is rarely taken advantage of. I know Bryant and I would do everything together, from grocery shopping, cooking, watching TV, movies and running errands, just to name a few. He loved Chinese food so we made that restaurant visit often. In June 2007, I traveled to Memphis with my youngest son Carson to watch Bryant play in one of his high school baseball games. I hadn't seen Bryant play since April and it's simply amazing what a difference two months can make in sports. I knew my son looked bigger and stronger on that field.

On that particular day, I wanted to take lots of pictures at his game for some reason. I stood mainly at the fence with my son Carson while my daughter sat in the stands talking to old friends. I took pictures from every angle I could manage. Bryant looked at me strangely at one point like he was saying, ''Why are you taking so many pictures?'' even though I had always been a picture-taking fool and all of friends always counted on me to be the snap photographer at most get-togethers. But, for some reason, I just kept taking pictures that day. Bryant played so well and looked so great on the field, and I was having so much fun.

Our next visit was in July 2007, and Bryant also would come to Louisiana and visit between regular season and fall season baseball. They normally only got two weeks off and we always planned our lives and vacation around his time off from baseball. It was the 4th of July and Bryant loved fireworks. I was never crazy about buying small sticks of fire and handing them to my child, but, again, as parents we do whatever we can to make our kids happy.

I had just landed a great job with Masimo a medical equipment company, in April 2007, and would be returning home from a training session July 3, 2007. I was super excited about flying in from California and knowing Bryant would be there when I got home made it even more of an exciting of a trip.

I had not seen Bryant in three weeks. I remember he called me while I was waiting to leave the airport and he asked me, "How do I get on the interstate?" I was confused because he drove that route so many times. He said, "I forgot I had senior pictures today, so I packed my stuff and wanted to leave from the studio."

I couldn't wait to see those pictures. My son was very handsome and could be very shy about how cute he was, too. I told him how to get on the interstate from Germantown, Tennessee where the photography studio was located and then I ran to catch my plane. I got home late that night -- around 10 pm -- after flying all day and to my great pleasure there everyone was, waiting for me to arrive. My youngest was all curled up on his brother, where he was most of the time when Bryant was here, and there was my husband, smiling in relief that I was home safely. The next few days, July 3-8, 2007, were simply great. We went to get Bryant's senior ring sized. And, of course, he wanted yet another truck accessory, so nerf bars were next on his list-- and being the great guy Wendell is, he wanted to have them put on Bryant's truck right away, which would be a belated birthday gift. That was Wendell's justification, anyway.

We ran so many errands, went to the movies, and went out to eat wherever Bryant wanted, visited our friends the St. Pierre's and shot lots of fireworks. I knew Sunday was coming and Bryant would have to leave for Tennessee to start baseball practice on Monday and that I would be headed back to California for a final week of training with my new job. I didn't want our time together to end. I remember Bryant packing to leave that Sunday. He kept finding reasons to delay his leaving. He was stalling. We talked about our beach vacation that would be in just two weeks and then he sat back on the couch and started playing with his little brother again. I told him it might be best because it was getting so late – for him to stay one more night with us and leave on Monday instead, when I was leaving out for California. As much as it seemed like he didn't want to leave, Bryant said it was time for him to go. ''No, I don't want to miss any practice.''

I finally told him he needed to get on the road for his six-hour drive. I never liked him leaving past 2 pm, so he wouldn't have to drive at night. It was already 4 pm and he was still playing. He finally got up and said, "I better go now.''

"Ok," I said, "but one last picture." Both my sons laid on their sides in ideal positions and I snapped one last picture. It was so cute of both of them.

I walked Bryant out to his truck and got my big hugs, but for some reason I just couldn't bring myself to walk off.

"Bryant, be very careful, you know Mommy can't live without you," and off he went. Little did I know I would be doing just that. I walked inside and I immediately had that same old uneasy feeling Mothers tend to get. I picked up the phone and called Bryant. I told him to call me when he got to his usual halfway spot where he stopped for gas. As I cleaned up around the house from a playful few days, I couldn't shake that feeling. I called him again to see where he was. ''Mom, I am fine! I will call you in a couple of hours when I stop.''

I found myself calling him every hour for the next six hours just to make sure he was safe.

Finally, when Bryant turned down his Dad's street, he called me to say he was back and would call me tomorrow. I knew I would be flying all day myself so I told Bryant I would call him as soon as I could.

CHAPTER 7

✼

Busy, Busy, Busy

That next week, Monday, Tuesday and Wednesday were long training days and with the time change from Louisiana to California, it made the days seem even longer for me. On Wednesday July 11, 2007, after a long day, I went to dinner with a few co-workers before returning to my hotel. I didn't realize how late it was. It was 10pm in California but that meant it was midnight in Memphis. I thought about calling my daughter too, who was vacationing in Houston, Texas with a few old sorority sisters, but I knew she was going to a concert and it was already midnight there, too. I normally never went a whole day without talking or texting my kids but the day had just slipped away. I sat watching TV for a few minutes when suddenly I felt short a breath. I was thinking, "What's wrong with me?" I stood up to walk around my hotel room. The feeling would not go away. I was so nervous, sweating, and I was short of breath. I was having a panic attack of some sort.

I wanted to pick up the phone and call my husband and kids to make sure everything was all right, but I glanced over at the clock and I remember it was 10:50 pm, that meant almost 1 in the morning where my family was. If I called any of them at that hour I knew it would scare them. After only what I can guess was about five minutes, I calmed down. I felt like I was jumping out of my skin. It was scary. I didn't know if I was having a panic attack, a heart attack or what was happening. I curled up and laid down on the bed to try to relax. I remember falling asleep, after trying to calm my sudden angst by thinking about how I only had two more short days of training to go and then I could plan our annual family beach trip. Knowing I would be together with my whole family on the beach again soon calmed me down. I fell asleep.

CHAPTER 8

❋

Worst Day of my Life

I've always heard the expressions, "that was the worst call you could ever receive" or "if my phone rings in the middle of the night, I would panic." I truly don't remember a lot after I picked up the phone at 2:21 a.m. California time to hear my husband sobbing and saying, "It's bad; it's Bryant!" "Don't tell me!" I screamed, and before I could take my next breath, Wendell sobbed, "He didn't make it!" For the next few minutes, I felt an empty feeling in my gut, my body felt weak. I shriveled up inside myself. All I could say is, "Where is my son?" Those few minutes were the longest, loneliest, weakest and most heart-crushing moments of my life. It actually frustrates me to try to explain the feelings you have when you hear your child is gone. There are no earthly words to describe a feeling of this magnitude.

I don't remember much else of the conversation, or if we just cried, but I had the energy to know I needed to get to my son as fast as I could. I called my co-worker who was also in training with me and the only thing I could muster to say was, "Come to room now!" John knocked on my hotel door within a minute. I told him the best I could manage that I had just gotten a call; that Wendell told me my son had died in an auto accident. I told John I needed his help getting on a plane. Without hesitation John said, "you pack, get dressed and I will take care of getting you on a plane." I think I walked in circles for a few minutes, but I managed to get dressed quickly and off we went.

We were headed to Memphis, but I had no idea where I was going or how to get there. John had called our company's emergency travel number and managed to get me on the first flight from LAX to Memphis, which was at about 5 a.m. I had not flown into LAX and didn't realize that we would have an hour or so commute to the airport from our hotel. I remember being on the passenger side in the car while John drove quietly but quickly. We didn't have much traffic at 3 in the morning, so we got to the airport on time. I imagined to myself all kinds of things that must have happened, but I never really thought Bryant was 100 percent gone. I remember thinking it was possible he could be gone, but it was also possible that one of his friends had borrowed his truck and they found Bryant's wallet and only thought it was Bryant.

Maybe my ex-husband was confused when he called my husband to tell him this news, just misunderstood and Bryant was seriously injured but not gone. I still have a hard time using the word "dead," and you will read me referring to my son as passed or gone, not "dead." I cried some more; I couldn't quit. I called my best friend of 25 years who lived in Louisiana. I also called my friend Julie, and my friend Pam, but I couldn't call my sister, my mother or my daughter. I knew that my husband had called my sister and I remembered my husband telling me my ex-husband had already booked a flight for my daughter from Houston, but calling my mother would have to come from someone else. I just couldn't do it. I don't know why; I think hearing her pain on the phone would confirm what I was trying to avoid. We arrived at LAX and John made sure I made it through security. I just walked in a fog to my gate. I say a fog because I really felt the world around me had blurred and I was the only person you could see. I sat at the gate waiting to board, crying so hard that it kept taking my breath away and every few minutes I would have to take a deep breath in order to stay alive.

A beautiful woman and whom I later learned was her 18-year-old daughter approached me from across the seating area at the gate and asked if I was ok? I immediately said, ''No! I was just told my son was killed few hours ago in a car wreck and I am going to Memphis to be with him.'' The woman dropped to her knees and put her hands on my shoulder and cried with me and kept saying, "I'm so sorry.'' It was time to board and I believe this woman must have told the flight attendants what was happening because they all looked at me as if they wanted to cry with me but they had to hold back the tears and board the plane.

I sat there on the plane just crying while people walked by me either staring or trying desperately to avoid eye contact. The lady across the aisle seat from mine asked me if I wanted to talk because she had lost her mother just four months ago and she had since gone through grief counseling. I remember thinking I didn't want to talk about Bryant anymore like he was gone because this could possibly be a case of mistaken identity. I knew this kind of thing had happened before and maybe – just maybe -- there was more than one person in that truck and Bryant was just injured. That flight from LAX took hours. I was in agony the whole time but still I kept feeling like I had someone watching over me or protecting me. I don't know exactly how to explain it except to say I knew deep in my heart Bryant had died and was holding me throughout that entire flight. When we landed in Memphis, I don't remember getting off the plane and I don't recall getting my luggage even though I know I did. All I could focus on; all I could do was keep telling myself that I need to get to my son. My friend Pam who lived in Memphis was at the airport to get me and she told me Kristina would be landing any minute from Houston. I hadn't spoken to my daughter yet so I called her to see where she was and where she would be waiting for us. I remember seeing Kristina walking, pacing, and looking lost.

She had no luggage with her and had boarded the plane in Houston completely forgetting to even get her luggage out of her friend's truck. Here she was with only the clothes on her back and she didn't even know it, or care. She was crying and looked like I felt. By the time we left the airport, my husband, my youngest son Carson, my sister Carla and my nephew Holden had made the almost six-hour drive to Memphis. Their plan was to meet at Pam's where we ended up living for the next seven days. I remember driving to my ex-husband's house. He was now remarried to a woman that I didn't really know and what I did know of her I didn't like and at this moment it would not have taken much for me to go crazy. I felt completely lost. All I could think and say was, "Where is my son?" My ex-husband spoke to the funeral home person who said Bryant was being transported to there from the morgue. It was only at that moment that I felt a complete helplessness.

I realized for the first time right then at that very moment that I could do nothing to help my son. How could he be on his way to a funeral home? What did they do to him at the morgue? Who has touched my son? He was so shy, and who touched him? I was angry. My ex-husband said Bryant wasn't ready to be seen. I looked at my husband and said, "Do something!" Wendell, being the protective type, went into motion and the people gave in. They said we could go see Bryant briefly, but I remember thinking, if at all possible, I would spend the night next to him. I felt like a complete stranger walking into the room where Bryant was; it was like I was violating someone's privacy that I didn't know. He was laying there, his hair somewhat damp from where they had washed him. He looked like he was asleep. He didn't look like someone who had been killed in a car wreck. I don't even know what that is sup- posed to look like really, but it was not at all as I pictured. Bryant had a small cut on his ear, which was still slowly bleeding. He also had a cut over his brow and a gash on his arm that looked like it was open at some point. I could only keep dapping his ear, as if I were caring for him in some way because he was bleeding. I don't know what I was sup-posed to do besides cry. I couldn't stop crying. I wanted to lay with him. I wanted to scream. I wanted to be so mad, but all I could do was cry. My beautiful boy, who I felt more joy from than anything else on this earth, was laying on a metal stretcher in a hospital gown with no heart beat and no breath. What was I supposed to do?

I kept asking myself. How do I do this? How do I walk out of this room or where do I go from here? His sister Kristina wouldn't come to the funeral home. I wish so badly to this day she had seen him so peaceful on that day. But she couldn't bear to see him and I under-stood why. Seeing her brother like that would make this tragedy all too real to her and she refused to make any of this real at all. I didn't realize then that my daughter was shutting down and this would af-fect her for years to come. After I don't recall how long, we left and drove back to Pam's where so many people had already started gath-ering for days of lost feelings and confusion.

CHAPTER 9

※

Baseball Memorial
July 12, 2007

T hat evening word had spread so quickly all over and it seemed like everyone was grieving; so many were in need of some news or direction. Someone called together a memorial that evening at the high school on the baseball field. By word of mouth, in only about eight hours, hundreds of teachers, coaches, parents, friends and family gathered at Cordova High School on the baseball field where my son played first base, the place where Bryant felt most at home in this world The baseball field was by far Bryant's most favorite place on earth. It was like his sanctuary. The Cordova High baseball head coach spoke to the shocked crowd and many people gathered on the field where a bouquet of yellow flowers sat on first base. Who brought those? Who gathered all these people?

So many questions . . . yet I still felt my son's presence all around me. I felt an inner comfort, as strange as that might sound, almost like a shield of protection. This day had been the longest day of my life from the wake-up call, the more than three- hour flight, then the reality of seeing my son lying on a table in a funeral home, and now a baseball field memorial. But I was not tired at all. I even remember thinking I would probably never sleep again. By this time, so many friends were there and caring for my needs had become the only way they felt needed or useful. My friend Pam, who lived in Memphis, opened her house up to my family and any friends who would sleep and eat there for the next several days. Finally, I saw my parents, who had driven in from south Arkansas.

They were weeping so much that I began to worry about my Dad. I thought, "I don't know if they can take this pain. "The team gathered in a circle as they did before each game. They put their hands together. The head coach asked Carson, my youngest and Bryant's brother, to stand in for Bryant. I still have no idea how any of this will impact Carson later in life, but everyone made sure to include him whenever possible. All of Bryant's friends knew how special his little brother was to him. Bryant and Carson, although 10 years apart, had a special bond from the moment of Carson's birth. Bryant was a hero to Carson and Carson was a little brother that Bryant felt obligated to love and protect. I stood alone in the midst of all these people on first base in despair and total disbelief. It was not long after the memorial that one of Bryant's classmates, Alec Ogg, wrote and recorded a song "#35" in Bryant's memory from the experience that day at the baseball field.

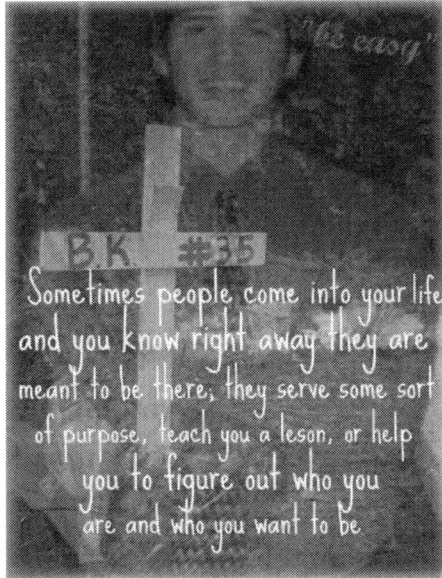

"be easy"

BK #35

Sometimes people come into your life and you know right away they are meant to be there; they serve some sort of purpose, teach you a leson, or help you to figure out who you are and who you want to be

CHAPTER 10

❊

July 12, 2007

I knew today would be a day I would never forget yet somehow it's all a blur. I think back about that day and even now I see glimpses of reality and confusion like it was a nightmare and not really real at all. I had to go to the funeral home and pick out a coffin, flowers and a burial site. Who does this? I kept thinking that over and over, and I might have even said it a time or two out loud. This is not real; I should be picking out clothes and making our annual vacation plans, but not this.

I remember seeing this silver coffin that we agreed on and then seeing the flowers. When the funeral home director asks a parent what type and color flowers would you like on your son's coffin you just answer like it's a make believe question. "Red, I guess, maybe he wouldn't care for yellow." That was my answer. I don't know how you make these choices, but when they are staring you in the face, you just do it. We sat in a room around a conference table there was my husband and me, my parents were there, my long-time girlfriend Megan, Bryant's Dad and his wife at the time. We all sat there. They took us for a ride around the cemetery and asked us to pick a burial spot for my son. Each garden had a name and, as we drove, I thought about who these people are? Who buried them? Are there children here? Is there a teenager here somewhere? We drove slowly down winding paths and the funeral director said, "This is where the babies are." Babies? I never really thought much about who was buried in cemeteries or who had to go through this heartache just like me now, not until now. He continued talking and telling us the names of the gardens, "To the left is the garden of ''everlasting life,''" he said.

Right when he said that, "everlasting life," it was like Bryant grabbed my arm and said, "Right here, Mom! This is where I want to be." It actually shook my insides I felt it so strongly. ''Right here!'' I said it OUTLOUD. "I want my son here in this garden across from the babies." Bryant loved kids so much and was always the one to have a posse of kids around him playing whenever the situation arose. From there, we drove back to the funeral home and other little details were taken care of, but I don't remember much about it or maybe I do but just choose to forget. I know we decided on the silver coffin, red roses and we picked out four bronze baseball gloves and baseballs that would attach to each corner of the coffin. I know visitation plans were made, but I have no idea who planned everything. The bronze gloves and balls would later be removed and given to the family as keepsake memories. I know we had been there for about five hours and, at one point, I got sick to my stomach and my husband, Wendell told me right away, "It's time to go, you've had enough.''

Back at Pam's, it seemed like more people had begun arriving, and so did a lot of food. Pam was running around organizing. My friend Megan had gone with me to the funeral home, along with my husband and my parents, so they were all exhausted both emotionally and physically. It seemed Carson was being showered with attention and, for the first time in my life, details and organizing were all being done while I sat there numb and in a fog. Bryant had gone and had his senior pictures taken right before he came to my house for the 4th of July and now the photographer was calling asking us if we wanted the pictures for the funeral. We drove to the studio. She came right out to meet us-- a sweet lady with a smile that appeared so nervous. ''We did these for you," she said. She handed me three large photos of my son. In one, Bryant wore his cap and gown, in one he was in a tux and in the other he was dressed in his casual clothes. The pictures were all on boards and ready for frames. My heart dropped into my stomach. I felt appreciative yet ripped up all inside all over again when I looked at the pictures.

He was so beautiful and I knew he would've loved these pictures. She gave me a CD of all his pictures and she steadfastly refused to take any form of payment. The word of my son's death had been on the news several times. Bryant was big news all over town because he was an honor roll student and an athlete with a tragic story. It was among the biggest news in town. I over- heard at least one TV broad-cast. Just listening to the story and then reading it in the paper, I felt mentally distant from it. I wanted to feel sorry for this child's mother but then I kept realizing the mother of this child on the news was, in fact, me. I must have asked myself a hundred times, how did this happen? My husband, a typical police officer, wanted answers. Wendell's family would be here soon from Kentucky, I had friends driving up from Louisiana and my extended family from Arkansas would be on their way. I don't know how everyone knew where to go or what to do, because I know I hadn't told them.

My friends had become an extension of myself, working hard to do to the work that I just couldn't do. I have never felt so helpless, so worthless and so cut off from reality in my entire life. I prayed for my son with every breath, but knowing all along where he was – in Heaven -- still brought me no immediate comfort at that time. My son had been raised in church and he was saved. I knew God had taken him, but why? Why would it be more important to have him in heaven than here with me? My son was so smart and was considering becoming a doctor. We had just talked about his future and his plans a few days ago. He would've been starting his senior year soon and he had so many questions and ideas. We talked about the Marines and tattoos. We had our beach trip plans . . . but never this -- this was not in our plans and why would God take him away from so many people who adored him? I walked around in circles wherever we went. Things that seem so easy, like going to the store to buy frames, were painstaking and seemed to take forever. Thank God for Pam, Tracie, and for my sister Carla and Lisa, who made sure the perfect pictures were displayed.

Tracie came over with her photo printer and away she went printing and cutting to perfection. Thank God for my loving sister who had to go shopping to buy clothes for my husband and son. Wendell had left Louisiana in such a rush he didn't think to pack much of anything. He drove up with my sister and they told me for six hours, other than a phone conversation or two with the state trooper from Tennessee, the car remained quiet and everyone was speechless. We later met with the officer to collect Bryant's belongings and I remember like it was yesterday. He looked me in the eye and said, "Your son was not wearing his seatbelt.'' I felt angry. "How could you tell me that, when I know better?'' I replied. "Trust me, Ma'am, he was not wearing his seatbelt.''

He always wore his seatbelt. He placed the shoulder strap behind him on many occasions, and I would fuss at him, but he always had his lap band on.'' All the details of the accident given to us one sentence at a time started bringing up more questions in my mind. I wanted someone to blame, wanted to get mad at someone, anyone! Bryant's phone was found in his jean pocket so he wasn't on the phone like many had thought. Was someone calling him and he was trying to answer his phone? Could someone have driven into his lane? The officer began to explain the scene and accident scenario to my husband and all I wanted to do was shut him out. Walking back to my car, where I sat and waited to leave felt like an eternity. We had Bryant's baseball bag, guitar and we needed to go to the wrecking company to look through his truck. I just sat, while the car moved, my husband driving on a mission to find answers. Going through the mangled truck, shifting through glass and debris, I asked Wendell why I was even doing this. I know that anything of Bryant's that I touched seemed to place him right there with me. I wanted to talk about him, talk about the accident, look through his things and just feel. I never saw his clothes until my friends brought them to me already washed. I wanted to be angry for a split second that they had washed Bryant's smell off without asking, but I knew by the look on their face they did it to wash away what I didn't need to see.

His shirt and jeans were perfect except for a few stains, so why were they not cut into pieces? I kept thinking, a thousand questions running through my mind. If they had tried to resuscitate him then why were his clothes intact? It seemed that everything brought more questions, but I had no answers. I brought up the question about his clothes to one of my girlfriends who also is a nurse. Sherrion hesitated but then muscled through it. She reminded me that when we saw him at the funeral home, Bryant's neck had a black and blue bruise on it, one that circled his neck. He must have broken his neck and "they knew that when they got to the site,'' she said. In all my years of nursing a lot of the details still do not sit right with me. How do you as EMS arrive at a crash site and assume resuscitation is not needed or will do no good? This question will only be answered in heaven, because all the explanations I have been given over the years as a registered nurse just continue to haunt me to this day. I guess I will have to wait for some answers, and I suppose other questions just don't need to ever be answered. I guess.

CHAPTER 11

✺

July 14, 2007

I woke up with little sleep and wondering who chose Sunday as visitation and Monday for a burial. I wanted this over, but at the same time I wanted to prolong it because I didn't want to let Bryant go. I still felt him as though he were with me in some inexplicable way. Bryant's friends stopped by one after another, some finding comfort in telling stories about Bryant, others just sitting and listening to others telling stories. At times, we found ourselves laughing, reminiscing over how funny Bryant was and the stories they were telling me.

How you could laugh right now, I would think to myself, but it was easy to laugh when someone was telling on your child. The story about Bryant's class ring sums up both his intelligence and wit. Sean, Bryant's best friend for many years, tells the story of how one night Bryant and a few friends went to a party in the woods, where he probably had no place being. The next day, after realizing his expensive senior class ring had fallen off his finger somewhere in the woods, Bryant decided they should go rent a metal detector to find his ring. Knowing Bryant, he probably thought he would be in big trouble when he had to tell me he had lost his new senior class ring because we both knew how much that ring meant to him. He was so proud of his ring. And hearing this story it all made sense to me. By the time he came to visit me only a week before his accident, Bryant was so insistent that we go have his ring sized to fit. Bryant had found his ring with the metal detector he rented that day, and when he got to my house he repeated to me several times, "You know mom, this ring is a little big and I would hate to lose it, so can we go get it fixed?" Of course, he never mentioned he had lost it in the woods during a party and then found after recruiting a band of friends to scour the grounds with a rented metal detector. The day seemed endless and I felt at times I was the only person in the room even while being surrounded by so many caring people. Losing Bryant put me in such a lonely place.

I wondered how I was supposed to be acting. What was I supposed to do now; how do I go on and live without my joy? I don't remember much about that day except that there was so much food. I remember, too, that people would whisper around me and that so many people just kept coming over to me, crying and hugging me, as well as each other.

Nobody knows what to say in a time like this. I never put much thought into a Mom losing a child before this happened because as Moms we simply don't want to go there. We don't want to think about those things. We even say in conversation, ''I can't imagine," and I heard that said so many times during that whole week that I wanted to climb on the roof and scream, ''Well, I can imagine and I don't want to imagine…take this AWAY from me.'' Wendell wanting to drive by the crash site at first made me angry. Why would anyone want to do that? I know now that he was searching for comfort, and I found myself searching for comforting, as well. The TV news must have aired my son's crash a half a dozen times and I know I must have heard it over and over. I saw it online, on the TV and in every newspaper we saw. It was real, but it wasn't.

CHAPTER 12

✳

July 15, 2007

T he amount of people in Pam's house was unbelievable and today was visitation. There were so many coming and going I don't really know who stayed over or who slept where. Everyone wanting to feed me somehow gave them comfort in wanting to help and get past their feelings of helplessness. I know now that people don't know what to do for you. I know now they just want to offer you comfort in some way, so my advice: let them serve you in whatever way you need. But how do you prepare yourself to greet so many people when all you want to do is get in the coffin and lay with your child? Arriving at the funeral home, just wanting to touch him and keep my hands on him, to never let him go was my only instinct. After standing by him, after playing with his hair for a long while, I was given a stool and told to sit down. I was okay with that because I could stay right where I wanted to be. I refused to move.

I saw people and heard voices but I was not in a mental state to respond to them nor to carry on any semblance of a conversation. A gentleman approached me and extended his hand then introduced himself as Bryant's third grade baseball umpire. He said he had umped many of Bryant's baseball games back then. Third grade. I didn't think much about him at the time, but later on the thought hit me: that was almost 10 years prior; what an honor to have so many adults think so highly of your child. "Did I recognize this when he was alive?" I asked myself this question and rolled it over in my head several times. I questioned whether I knew how special my son was to other people, to so many other people. I knew how special he was to me, but I could not be sure I realized how and in what ways he touched so many lives in only 17 short years. The five hours I spent on a stool by Bryant seemed like five minutes when I was told it was time to go. I didn't know how to walk away. I wondered who was going to stay with him. I thought he might even be scared if he was left alone. I felt like a puppet sometimes being told what to do and when to do it.

This lack of having any semblance of control was nothing like me at all, but I know now this was my worst, most vulnerable state ever. The mental and the physical fatigue and weakness that takes over is frightening at the moment and even when you look back and remember. Is this the time when people lose their minds? Is this when people actually lose it, when someone goes crazy and does something they can never undo? I asked myself that many times. Still, through every bit of that seemingly never-ending traipse with the surreal and morbidly debilitating state, I always felt a very strong connection to my son; it was like he was walking with me, like he was sitting with me wherever I was led or ended up. Somehow, someway, in spite of my weakness, my mental frailties, my physical despondency and the grief that was actually paralyzing me, Bryant was giving me an inner peace. Somehow, even though I felt so much pain, numbness and seclusion because Bryant was gone, he was still there. Forget making sense of it because sense did not apply to what I was feeling. It was all so much deeper than that.

CHAPTER 13

✳

July 16, 2007

Today I bury my child. I don't know how this has happened or why and I feel sick.

The ceremony is so hard for me to recount today, but I do remember my daughter and Sean speaking and I vividly remember thinking. "How is she getting through this?" She was such a wreck yesterday and her friends had to drag her up to see her brother. I really believe Bryant held her hand, and I really believe that to this day he holds her hand when she doesn't even know it. We played Bryant's kind of music and, as a matter of fact; mostly his close friends and family arranged the entire funeral.

Friends gathered pictures of Bryant because all of my photos were at home in Louisiana since I had flown directly into Memphis from California. I had nothing but what was in my suitcase. Somehow, I managed to say a poem while standing beside my son's casket, but I have no idea what I said exactly. I wanted to crawl into the casket with him and scream out loud at the same time. I have never felt so lonely and abandoned. I couldn't function, and I could have gone to a dark place and never come back.

This was my Bryant in that silver coffin with red rose's covering the top, a bronze baseball glove and ball on each corner. I was going through the motions but not really believing what was happening around me at all. I had so many thoughts running through my head but none of them made any sense. There I am looking at my parents, my children, at my husband and the hundreds of people in attendance and I remember I just couldn't register what was really happening. There was still, however, an unexplainable comfort inside me. I felt it. I couldn't have begun to explain it then, and I can hardly identify with it now, but I remember it was there.

It was the only thing keeping me going. It wasn't until after the funeral when so many people who had come in from out of town were saying good-bye that I no longer felt that comfort I had felt. I felt like I had just said good-bye to my Bryant and it was so real at that moment. I didn't want to leave him but, again, someone who was just trying to help dragged me away. I don't know where my fighter spirit had gone but I had no energy to argue. I was so depressed I couldn't resist anyone telling me what to do. I call myself strong willed but I was nothing more than a shell of person by then. I couldn't muster a fight inside and what remnant of life I had left felt like it was leaking out of my pores. Back at Pam's, Megan realized it was her birthday. She had actually forgotten that it was her birthday and so had I. We never discussed it until a year later, but my best friend's birthday will forever be on the anniversary of the burial of my son Bryant.

CHAPTER 14

❈

Searching for Peace

In peace, some answers, brought little comfort and I looked for anything to give me some kind of some healing. I read sympathy cards over and over, looked for books, searched for psychics and sought out the counsel of preachers! I had to leave my son in the ground in Tennessee and drive back to Louisiana. It was the toughest things I have done, leaving him there. I wanted to escape my deep sorrow and to be released from my constant misery. Even with people telling you that he is in your heart now not in the ground, I felt so heavy.

I found myself gasping like I was running out of air to breathe. For weeks to come, I found what little comfort I could find only while lying in my bed or through eating food. My youngest son was so sad, and I didn't want him to see me cry all the time, but how do you just turn it off? Carson lost his big brother and his hero. My daughter lost her little brother and her best friend. My husband, who loved Bryant like his own and had ever since Bryant was 8, grieved like nothing he had ever experienced before. And me? I was of no use to anyone anymore I know how it feels to have those oppressive negative feelings so deep and so heavy you know it's crushing you, when it is a battle just to step out of bed. I know how it feels when you feel like everyone around you seems happy and actually has the audacity to be going on with his or her everyday life – everyone but you. I know it's repulsive and how it makes you angry inside, how you feel like everyone around you is so selfish for not grieving with you.

The faintest memories stirred, the most remote sites, hard or soft sounds, old songs, new songs, and even the smells in the air you breathe can be overwhelming. There are still to this day periods of time leading up to holidays, birthdays, and even Mother's Day, which can actually be worse experiences for me than the day Bryant died itself. I had so much anxiety over the first few months – anxiety about how I was going to function as a mother, sister, friend, daughter and wife. I needed to do something. But what? What could I do? What would Bryant want me to do? What does Bryant want me to do? My father, who adored Bryant, just happened to mention to me in passing one day, "You should have a scholarship in Bryant's name." It struck me. What a great idea! And, I remember thinking; this will keep my baby in the hearts and minds of loved ones and friends forever." I told Bryant's father and a few of his close friends, and away they went! The Bryant Kite Scholarship Fund was born. Bryant had an amazing group of friends and they all wanted so much to do something for him and they all felt so helpless over his death.

The night he passed away, Bryant had just left a group of friends and was on his way home when he crashed his truck. There was nothing any of his friends could have really done that night to prevent the accident, but still they all they struggled with the "what ifs" and "I should haves." It actually took me more than a year to accept the statement, "When God calls you home, it's just your time to go and your work here is done." I never wanted to hear that my precious son had nothing more to give on Earth at the tender age of 17. He loved life, loved his family and his friends meant so much to him I can't even begin to describe it. But, I can see now how Bryant touched so many in his short life, and how, even now, his memory continues to reach and teach others every single day. The Bryant Kite Scholarship Fund started with a simple Spring Festival only nine months after his death -- what would've been one month before his high school graduation. When Bryant died for the longest time it seemed, although I could actually manage a smile and feel pain all at the same time, I never really had any joy. I didn't see how I could ever be joyful again with Bryant gone. I couldn't fathom it. I actually felt that it was a selfish and self- centered act for a mother to be happy once her child has died. I know now, and so will you, that your child would cry in heaven if they knew how much pain you carried every second of your life. Realizing this never stops the tears, but finding some happiness in your new, normal life, in what is now your world, is not only okay, but also it is simply necessary for you to function.

The guilt of not being there to save him can leave me short of breath even today if I had not decided to forgive myself and to truly trust that God is in control. He was in control then and he is in control now. You can start small by just addressing the "elephant in the room," by acknowledging your loved one and including him or her in your gatherings by lighting a candle, making a toast in his or her honor, or sharing favorite memories and funny stories about them over dinner. It may be difficult to start these conversations but it will benefit everyone around you and help each of you heal, if only a little bit at a time. Remember as much as you may hurt, the memories, love and feelings of our child in our hearts can never be taken from us unless we let them. Allow yourself to live the life God has given you. Your child is not physically here on earth but he or she will forever be your child. I knew as hard as it was for me to do, it was so vitally important to Carson at the age of 7, having lost his bother and hero, that I accept the invitation to attend Cordova High School's homecoming game and speak at halftime. It had only been three short months, but Carson needed to be with Bryant's friends, and even though I didn't realize it at the time, I needed to talk about my son to anyone that would listen. So, it was in October 2007, the high school stadium was filled to capacity and I was surprised all the more by the crowd of tailgaters in the parking lot before the game. But it wasn't until a few gentlemen approached me and said, "Bryant always said we should tailgate like LSU before the games and nobody ever did until today," that I realized what was going on. My heart filled with pride because this was all for my Bryant and they knew, too, how special he was. Carson sat with Bryant's friend in the stands and was "one of the guys" just like his 17-year-old brother would've done. And Carson smiled and laughed for the first time in months. Bryant's friend Cam was the quarterback and he said before the game he was determined to win the game in Bryant's honor.

Cam dedicated this game to Bryant. Cam wore wristbands on each arm with Bryant's baseball number "35" and, on the very last play of the game, Cam, sporting those #35 wristbands, threw a perfect pass for a touchdown to complete a come from behind Homecoming win for Cordova High. Bryant was thrilled. So was Carson. And, so was I. The Cordova High homecoming game was bittersweet both for my son, Carson, and for me. I was asked to give a speech at half- time in the press box. On my way up the bleachers to press box just before half, I was approached by a lady with tears in her eyes who put her hand on my arm and said, "My son died too in a car wreck several years ago, and I wish I had the strength to speak freely about his memory.'' I wasn't sure if she was complimenting my courage or judging my strength, so I hugged and thanked her and continued up the stairs. The huge banner hanging from the press box in memory of both our sons put a small smile on my face.

Gathering my composure and praying for strength I began my speech over the microphone as everyone stood in the stands in si- lence.

My speech:
Bryant Kite Standup guy in a bow down world

When I think of my son, I think of a young man that is truly a mother's dream. Bryant was a typical teen that discovered what it meant to study, earn money, drive for the first time, get a girlfriend, hang out with friends, go to Friday night parties, live with divorced parents, play serious sports, schedule vacations, play a guitar, be a friend, be a son, be a hero to a little brother and pick on a big sister, but love her unconditionally. Bryant lived his life filled with what and who he loved. He knew that it's not the quantity of one's life that is important, but the quality of your life that is real. This is why it's possible for a 17-year- old to live more fully and touch more lives than a person who has lived to his eighties.

Bryant is much like Daniel in the Bible; he was a leader and a stand up person, even when others were not. Bryant was a young man of integrity and character. A crisis doesn't make character; it reveals character and Bryant stayed strong even in the toughest situations. He was a young man of conviction and he knew his decisions today would define him tomorrow. He was a young man of courage and he faced even the toughest times and decisions with respect. He was committed. Keeping a commitment and his word was a lifestyle for him. He was accountable for his actions and showed great compassion. He never forgot his friends and family no matter what was going on in his life. Most people are like stained glass windows.

They sparkle and shine when the sun is out, but when the darkness sets in; their true beauty is revealed only if there is a light from with- in. Bryant had a light from within that everyone could see. He was a light that many of us were drown to in our dark and sad times. He was the king in my house and Wendell often joked that when "Bryant's here everyone else takes a back- seat". Bryant was affectionate, passionate, patient and kind. He felt everyone's pain and would try to save you from hurt if he could. I cry out of selfishness for my boy every day, wanting him to be here and yet knowing God is using him as an angel in all our lives.

Thank you boys for being a good friend to my angel.

Thank you Libby for taking my angel to church.

Thank you Carson for always showing Bryant your sweetheart.

Remember to be a light that shines through in the dark times; "Be Bryant like" and be a stand up person in a bow down world.

CHAPTER 15

The Strength to Get Up Each Day

A nd we know that God causes all things to work together for good to those who love God, to those who are called according to His purpose. – Romans 8:28 (NASB)

Through days of intense pain, I will try to think about how God uses every situation and tragedy for the good. How can this be good? Romans 8:28 clearly says "God causes all things to work together for good. . ." All things include the untimely passing of a child or loved one, as incredible as they may seem, but that's where faith comes in.

When I look back now, I see how many people God used to get me through and now I see how this has impacted their lives for the good, too. Moving through the depression I also had to deal with others wanting to help me in some way. It's not easy; it's not fun. I really prefer to be the person helping and in control, so this alone was extremely difficult for me to deal with. I had to graciously accept their offers to help while wanting to just curl up in a ball and cry out to Bryant to come back home. Sometimes the pain and depression became so bad it scared me and I couldn't even breathe. Sometimes when I really didn't want to cry at all the tears would just flow down my face like a water fall. I would hear Satan at times trying to lie to me, telling me to be angry with God, but I know Satan comes only to lie, to steal, kill and destroy our lives. In this case, Satan was trying to take any ounce of joy and turn it into anger and a feeling of hopelessness. I think back and I see clearly now how much time I wasted feeling sorry for myself, and how much I wished Bryant was here, instead of focusing on the good memories of my son and allowing God to show me purpose. I occasionally will resort back to how life would've been had none of this happened. But in reality it's all God's plan; we just don't have all the answers.

I have had so many reasons to bring the pain back again and I believe that's normal when we are trying to adjust to our "new normal" life. When Bryant's friends and classmates were graduating in May 2008 and I stood on that stage knowing my son was not out there, and I gazed in the audience I could see their eyes full of tears and saddened hearts, I mourned for him all over again. You will have days that flood your thoughts with memories but it's in these times we have to find inner strength to have those thoughts and then get back to living. I have learned through the death of my son that I received two wake-up calls. The first wake-up call was from my husband telling me of Bryant's death. The second wake-up call was the truth of God's love and how he brings people into your life for a reason. God loves people through people. I have met so many who helped me. I have also been asked to reach out to other mothers who are suffering the loss of a child. I had a lot of serious reservations about reaching out to try to help another mother.

The first time I realized I could help someone else was when a co-worker called me from out of state and asked that I call his friend who was an absolute stranger to me. Evidently, she had lost a son as well and just wasn't able to cope even with the help of friends and family, and they felt she was getting worse, not better. I finally called her, although I stared at her number for an hour before I picked up the phone. I told her who I was and that I knew exactly what she was going through. I only heard silence and then I heard a sigh, "Finally, someone who really understands," she replied. We talked for more than an hour and when we hung up I realized reaching out to help her really just helped heal me. Grieving takes up 10 times the energy to get through a day. Exhaustion can be one of the hardest parts of grieving. I stayed in denial for six months, whether I needed medication or counseling, or both. I tried three different medications and nothing seemed to work. But counseling just wasn't something I was willing to try until six years after Bryant died and I can tell you that

I only wish I had swallowed my pride and gone much earlier. It may take you time to find the right person. I actually saw two counselors and my second choice helped me through so many questions I had in only three visits. This may not be the path for you, but I can truly say it did open my eyes to some of my feelings. As difficult as it may seem, there will be other people in your life that you will need to live for, whether it is a spouse, a child, family members or friends that are giving us encouragement and support. We have to accept our life now and this life is your "new normal." You will find other mothers that have lost children, although you feel like you're on a distant island all alone and nobody understands your pain, that nobody feels the way you do because your child was so special and you were so close, but there are other hurting mothers.

My son thought I hung the moon and I use to tease my family and tell them "don't you dare tell him any different". We were so close and had a loving relationship even though he didn't tell me everything; I know he respected me too much to ever disappoint me. I met a beautiful woman by the name Christy only four weeks after Bryant died and she told me how she had lost both her son and husband in a car accident and how it took her a year just to go back to work. Christy told me she managed her time by reading books. She told me to go buy her favorite book and as soon as I left her I went straight to the bookstore. I read that book and started a journal a few months later, not realizing at the time I was writing my own book and finding purpose.

CHAPTER 16

Journaling

Journal entry #1: My first Birthday without Bryant
November 12, 2007 8:32am:

Today marks four months since my son was taken from me. I can't say that the 12th of each month gets any easier for me, but I do know that Bryant is safe and with the Lord! I am told that I should celebrate Bryant's passing but I am not able to do that just yet. I have a song that I wanted to share with you that a dear old friend shared with me the day my son died. Treasure your family, be proud of your children and spend time with the friends that truly love and care for you. Life has no guarantees except for that one day when life promises to end. I live with no regrets for the way I raised my son. He was exceptional and I am proud of him every day of my life. Don't get bogged down with people or things that will bring emptiness. Work is necessary, but family and good friends are priceless!

November 12, 2007 7:40pm Four months without my son

I wake up; I go to sleep, and still no closer to an answer of why I have to be the mom that can only think about her son's hugs and kisses. My Bryant stood 6'1, brown hair, brown eyes, tan skin and a smile that caught more attention than any boy I know. He was my joy and my precious angel. I could buy Bryant a pair of shoes and he would appreciate it. He would drive to Louisiana and drive back to Tennessee and never ask you for gas money unless I remembered to give him cash. But he would never ask. Bryant sat on the couch next to me watching football and let me lie on his shoulder and never move, even if his arm was asleep. He made my day by just needing me to cook him breakfast. I miss him more than words could ever explain. You would have to feel my pain in order to understand what it's like to lose your precious child. I once only thought I knew what that must feel like. I was way off.

I believe God sends every person in our life to us for a purpose and not by accident. I do believe it was meant for me to meet Christy, who I have never seen again since that day. I look at some mothers and I see the pain on their face just standing in a room and think, is this how I look? Can everyone see my heart? I knew my son would want me to be the best I could be but that confidence came in time, not right away. You will find your own comfort, whether it's through establishing a scholarship in their name, placing a plaque on the wall at their school, having a quilt made from all their clothing or just any activity that consumes our time and keeps our mind busy. It could be reading "grief" books to survive, writing our thoughts in a journal, making crafts, playing the piano, listening to music, planting a garden, and walking along the beach, counseling, church or just praying. Looking for an outlet is completely normal, and finding a way to preserve a child's memory is also perfectly normal. You need to remember as a mother your grief is isolated to your role in your child's life and you must never forget how much love and joy you had for your child. But there are also so many others grieving for your child. Don't forget all the family/ friends that loved your child and shared their own memories and roles in each other's life. My son Carson is 14 years old now and I still don't know if we have seen all the effects he's going to have from losing his brother. Bryant was his hero and he was so proud of him. Carson was only 7 when he had to endure so much pain, pain that for the most part he couldn't even begin to understand. Here is my youngest son who went from playing baseball like his brother in the back yard just four days before he died to suddenly having no visible existence of him in his life. He has only memories of his brother. His favorite is the story he tells about when he fell asleep with fruit snacks in the bed and Bubby, as he called Bryant, woke up with gummy snacks all stuck to his leg hair. He laughs every time he tells the story.

It's so easy to compare your grief to others and, yes, it is different and deep, but don't dismiss or exclude the pain others have. Never lose sight of the awful fact that they're suffering, too. I wanted to keep Bryant everywhere in my house. I had a picture of Bryant literally on every wall and on every shelf of my house and nobody was going to touch his room if I had anything to do with it. It did take me some time to hear my family pleas to remove some of his pictures and stop making the house a Bryant shrine. I read somewhere that it's never a good idea after a child's death to make any big decisions or changes for at least one year. I totally agree with this.

I would not allow anyone to TOUCH ANYTHING in Bryant's room and I was not going to change his room no matter what. Then, after one year, I donated his bed to a family who had two sons and needed a bed for them. I turned Bryant's room into a guest room. I put all of his belongings into a very large enclosed bin and labeled it. I kept a lock of his hair and the keys to his truck that he wore on a lanyard in a drawer beside my bed and I still do. I have a few beautiful pictures of Bryant displayed in our home and his senior picture hangs in the center point of our house now as a memory of our angel and strength.

CHAPTER 17

Allow Yourself Peace in Grief

Grief can be very overwhelming and it leaves us with feeling of helplessness. Even with established stages of grief: anger, denial, bargaining, and acceptance, we still are unique individuals and we can experience so many different levels of pain. The first year you can experience all stages of grief but my experience is that not all stages last equally in amounts of time. No two people are alike in grief. I wish someone had told me about just some of the feelings that I would go through, that were possible, and I wish I had known then what I realize now. So, I hope sharing this experience will make peace of mind easier to find for you.

You will feel like your life is over and the world doesn't care about your child anymore. I can assure your life does go on even though you may not feel like you want it to. The life you will call your "New Normal" will slowly begin. You may find yourself sitting for hours and nothing gets done, but it's okay as long as you can continue to care for yourself and the others that truly need your attention.

No matter how bad a day feels, it is only one day. When you go to sleep crying, you will wake up with the power to make a choice on how you want to live that day. Wake up tomorrow and say out loud: Today I choose to live the way (name) would want me to. I choose to remember one happy memory. Grief comes and goes like a vicious roller coaster. One day you can talk about your child and the next day you can't speak or hear their name without having a total breakdown. This is all part of your new normal life. Don't forget, it's okay to cry. Do it often. But don't forget it's okay to laugh, too. Don't feel guilty for feeling positive emotions even when dealing with losing someone so precious to your heart. Monitor your self-talk for negative messages and replace them with positive ones. Even if you don't believe what you're saying, sending a healthy intention can work wonders.

Try to take good care of yourself by eating healthy and/or going to the gym even if you don't want to. This one is still a struggle for me and has been even though it's more than six years later. You may find that you're doing great for a few months but that you then resort back to your old depressive ways. It happens, but as long as you get back on track, you will be okay. Don't shut people out of your life or hide from them how you're feeling. You will lose relationships and gain relationships during your life's grief journey.

Some people will surprise you, for the good and for the bad, but remember those that love you can be hurt if you don't allow them to help you. Sometimes they don't know how to deal with their pain so they will reach out to you. Don't cut yourself off from their reach. They need your touch and you need theirs. Reach out to others. This can seem daunting, especially when you don't even have the energy to get out of bed. But keep the phone or computer handy and reach out as much as you can to those you love and trust. God will be there for you and it's okay to cry out to him. He will never, ever let you down. He will let you scream, cry, and question. Throw all your emotions at Him. He is near to the brokenhearted. Take time to truly remember the precious life you lost. Write about him or her, go back to all your memories with them in all the good times you had. It will help; this is how I started to heal. Dealing with the grief head on is better than running from it or denying it. Don't hide from the pain. If you do hide from it will fester and it will grow and it will consume you. It could turn into a worse issue than you ever intended. If family tells you it's time to get help, don't ignore them or worse get mad. Just go get help. You will ask "Why?" with no answers more times than you can count. What helps is prayer, asking God for mercy and strength. He will show you how to be strong.

He will provide strength. You may ask "How?" But it is probably better to ask not how did they die but how did they live? And, how can we honor them in memory. You will try to escape grief by getting busy. You will think that if you don't think about it, it'll just go away. This isn't really true. Take time to process and begin to heal. Food, liquor, drugs, hobbies, work, and other relationships will appear to take the pain away and give you peace. But if you are trying to use anything to numb the pain that can lead to other issues, danger or unhealthy lifestyle changes. I recommend you seek help immediately before it gets worse and consumes you. You may be asked, "How many children do you have?" It's okay to include your deceased child in that answer. After all, he or she is always your child. I typically answer by saying, "I have three children and my middle child passed away." I usually get shocked looks but I simply smile and continue the conversation.

If someone is uncomfortable that's not your issue, it's his or hers. It's okay to enjoy your life without feeling guilty about living. You are alive and your loved one would not want you crying all the time. It's okay to be angry as long as you can move past it. Get some sun.

Withdrawing to a dark room can only hinder your progress. Try to sit in the sunlight for a few minutes every day. Vitamin D has a direct impact on brain functioning, and sunlight is the prime source of vitamin D. Allow others to have a life, too, and have fun without you making them feel like they should be grieving. Every one grieves differently.

Depending on the circumstances of death you may find yourself wanting to blame others for your pain and this isn't healthy. Whether it is at the hand of another or in my son's case just a random accident with no one else involved, the pain is still there and the healing comes from God from within yourself and the strength you find in God. If you have other children, you need to continue to live strong for them. Don't compare their talents, personalities or dreams; just support them for being them and remember their loss is a pain you may not see for years to come.

CHAPTER 18

❋

5 Stages of Grief to Avoid Destruction

W HAT WOULD YOU DO IF YOU GOT THAT PHONE CALL, OR IF SOMEONE CLOSE TO YOU HEARD THESE WORDS "YOUR CHILD HAS DIED?"

THE 5 STAGES

DENIAL - Recognizing the stages of grief can help you by keeping you from believing you are alone or going crazy. There is no way to accelerate or sidestep the process of grieving; grief is a healing process your mind needs to go through. Verbal acknowledgement is the first step and the most difficult because you are admitting your child or loved one has died.

ANGER - Getting mad and blaming some- one, even God, is a natural reaction to such a tragedy. When you have moved on to the next stage, however, you may have destroyed a relationship you once valued. Keep your anger in control by using a punching bag, screaming into a pillow, crying out loud for as long as you need, then turn your anger into a passion. If your loved one or child was killed by a drunk driver you may want to join a support group and work to lobby newer stricter laws. If your loved one died of a horrible disease you can volunteer for support in raising funds for a cure. There are countless ways to turn your Grief into a gift of giving back.

BARGAINING - This is a trickiest of stages where your mind begins its creative work which can be good and bad. This stage can occur before a death if you have a sick child or loved one. You may find yourself focused on what you could have done differently in order to prevent the loss or change how it happened. You may also think about all the things that could have been and how wonderful life would have been if your child or loved one had not died. These thoughts may help you begin to accept the reality of it all but this is also where some of us may get stuck and unable to move further in the grief journey or begin to move slowly into depression. You may begin to have feelings that can also lead to guilt that interfere with healing. Nothing will change by harping on the "what ifs" or "only ifs," so use the bar- gaining stage to change you by showing a better appreciation for life and honor your child or loved one by being the best you can be for others.

DEPRESSION - Have no bargaining power left, our emotions begin to enter deeper level of emptiness and sadness. You feel like you don't care about much of anything and wish your life away. You may find simple daily activities are difficult or just not important like skipping the teeth brushing routine or just lying in bed because getting out of bed can be a huge burden. Your friends and family will try to help get you on a faster road to recovery in this stage, but there is no time limit on staging. I tried everything to move past depression but nothing worked. This may be the time to seek counseling or medication if your doctor prescribes it because it's important to know that this isn't a mental illness and you're not going nuts, yet it's a natural response to your loss. It's not a clinical depression we're experiencing, but rather bereavement and mourning, and the emotions of depression must be experienced in order to heal. We have to let ourselves feel the pain, sadness, hurt, loss, grief, and mourn. You may want to avoid isolation as much as possible. When a person is hurting, they often just want everyone to leave them alone. They build protective walls around themselves, not only to keep other people out, but also to guard against unwanted emotions. By not allowing yourself to cry or get mad you get stuck in depression and can't move forward to acceptance.

ACCEPTANCE - You may feel like saying you're in the stage of "acceptance" means you have to be "cured" or "all better" after burying your child or loved one, but this couldn't be further from the truth because it isn't the case at all. Your pain and the feeling that a part of you is missing will forever be a part of your life and what is referred to as your new normal life. Acceptance simply means you are ready to try something new to heal and move for- ward. It gives the word hope a new meaning. Most of us will feel a huge sense of guilt by admitting we are in the acceptance stage because we think others will view this as us being "over it" or we are being "unfair to our child or loved one." You may feel this might mean you didn't love your child enough, or that you're being disrespectful or cheating them in some way. When you accept your child or loved one is gone we are not saying anything at all except we are ready to move forward without this person and learn how to live our new normal life with this piece of our heart and our life in the physical world. Then, you can focus on how you want to remember your child or loved one in the way they would want to be remembered.

An outlet for grief -- a sport, a craft, a social club, exercising, writing these can all be active ways of pushing through your journey.

Wake-up call is to gain a better understanding of someone in the face of grief. Have you gone through all 5 stages of grief?

Here is a short checklist to help you or someone you know in their walk.

Can you admit that your child or loved one has died and your life will be forever changed by this loss?

Do you have the strength to identify your anger and express your anger in healthier ways that don't hurt yourself or other?

Are you able to share your pain and are you able to allow others to help you in your grief?

Can you understand that you cannot bring them back or do any- thing to change what has happened?

Have you found ways to channel your emotions in healthier ways or to have the ability to love and to beloved by others?

CHAPTER 19

❋

Holidays Can Be the Most Trying

The holidays, certain occasions, and even special events can be a very difficult time for those who are grieving. The holidays are a reminder of the people who should be at the holiday table, but are not. Their absence remains, even as the years pass. Of course, it does get easier; it is always a tough. It's important to realize that you don't have to do things the way you've always done them. It may be a good time to start some new traditions, this doesn't mean you're going to lose the old traditions; Address the "elephant in the room" by acknowledging your child or loved one and including him or her in your gathering by lighting a candle, making a toast in his or her honor, cooking their favorite dish or sharing favorite memories and funny stories about them. It may be difficult to start these conversations but it will benefit everyone around you and help each of you heal a little bit at a time. Remember to give "thanks" for what you had and what you still have… memories, love and feelings in our hearts can never be taken from us unless we allow it.

I found myself the first few Christmas's after losing my sweet Bryant looking for gifts for him when I was shopping for others. For a split second I would see something and think, "Bryant would love that." I still have moments of heartfelt sadness during the holidays. Sometimes, the days leading up to Thanksgiving or Christmas or worse than the actual holiday itself because the planning seems to linger on, everywhere you look you see joy, family gatherings and parties but someone is missing so how can I have joy or a party? How do I enjoy Mother's Day ever again when one of my children is gone? The anniversary of Bryant's death is always a reflection day of what could've been different and what he would be today. Why did the accident happen? How did the accident happen? Why Bryant? What did I do to deserve losing my son? After all these years, it's still not easy for me to relate what happened. My "New Normal Life" is a fact that dealing with these days and occasions will be with me until the day I die. I didn't want to be a member of this exclusive club of suffering mothers, who buried their child, but this is what I have to deal with, and I have realized I need to somehow find and live its purpose.

VACATIONS

Vacations can be very slow to heal. If your family had a favorite vacation spot that your child loved, going back there can bring on a flood of memories. Some of my most treasured memories are from our annual trips to the beach. I grew up in Baton Rouge, Louisiana and my parents always brought us kids to the Florida coast every year. I continued that tradition with my children and we went every year. We moved to Tennessee when Bryant was almost 2, so he grew up in Memphis. We traveled several times a year to Louisiana to visit family and friends. Every summer we planned a trip to Gulf Shores where we would vacation with all of my friends that I grew up with in Baton Rouge. I basically loved any and all beaches and Bryant loved them, too. He had every float, boogie board and sand board made. It really didn't matter how old he was, he always wanted to go to the beach and looked forward to it every year, every trip.

The day Bryant left to drive back from Louisiana to Tennessee four days before he died, we were discussing the best time to work in our family vacation beach trip. I loved the beach and named it my "happy place" because this was the only place I could go and totally relax and enjoy life with my kids, family and friends. The rich memories of so many beach trips with Bryant made vacationing there after Bryant passed away difficult at first. I would cry for hours, day and night when we got there. It wasn't until a couple of years later that I was laying on the beach in deep thought of how Bryant's life would've been had he not died that summer night when a voice popped in my head like someone was sitting next to me and said, "let this place give you peace because I am in my place of peace." "Ok, Bryant," I replied audibly and conversationally without even thinking or hesitating. Today the beach is my safe refuge of peace and I call it "my happy place." My family and friends know that no matter what happens I will make it to the beach every year because they know that at the beach I truly feel peaceful.

It's hard, it escapes logic, and the demons that want to deny you peace and joy are real, but you have to listen to your heart. God lives in your heart once you accept Him and surrender your life to Him. But that doesn't mean His still voice is at want of being drowned out by negativity both self-cultivated and cast upon us by the fiery darts of the adversary. Your child wants you in a place of utter peace. Find your refuge even if it's sitting on the back porch. Whatever gives you some sort of peace and is a healthy ways of relaxing, you need to cultivate and guard that for yourself.

There may always be places and situations you may never be able to go or visit because you can't get past the pain. I love my son's friends and I loved to watch him play baseball, but for me going back to the baseball field at his high school is extremely difficult. His friends called everyone to gather on first base at Cordova High School one year after Bryant died. They called me in Louisiana and asked me to come. I had a sudden feeling of anxiety. I remember that day because I was sitting with my friend Angela who was a friend God had sent to be a part of my life four months after Bryant died. I told her I didn't think I could go and that the long drive by myself to Memphis would be dreadful. Without hesitation she replied, "I think you need to go and I will take you." Angela did just that.

Together, we made that journey to Memphis, and she stood on that field with me, drove me to Bryant's gravesite and sat with me while I cried. She never said one word, just cried with me.

God will send you a new friendship when you need it and when it's the perfect timing for it. We have helped each other in times of need ever since. Every year my sweet friends from both Louisiana and Tennessee join together at our annual 5K run to honor Bryant and celebrate his life. The bond and friendship I have with my sister is one that simply can't be shaken. Carla has never missed an annual 5K run. She is solid and strong and I have and can count on her in my darkest hours. There is no doubt, you will go through so many life changes, but I have come to know that every change brings me closer to God's plan. Relationships can be just another life changing situation after the death of a child or loved one. It's amazing how differently people respond after a death. You may have episodes where you will want to just distance yourself from others. I person-ally didn't want any encouragement from others; I just wanted my son back. You will lose and gain friendships along the way. You will have some people that will surprise you for the good and some who will for the bad. You may have a friend from the past resurface and friends you will meet in the months after the death of your child or loved one that you know the minute you meet them that God has sent them into your life for a reason and for the purpose of healing in many ways. I lay in bed many a day, sometimes day after day, unable to function mentally, and sometimes physically, after I buried Bryant. Some days I felt completely incapacitated and I didn't want to do anything at all. My daily torment was if my eyes were open I was crying or just feeling pain unbearable. Some people can't handle dealing with someone in such deep despair no matter how close you were before. There are marriages that can't make it through a death of a child. I was divorced from Bryant's Dad but had been remarried to my husband Wendell since Bryant was 9. You may fight and dis- agree for many rea- sons but the main cause for argument I hear time and again is over how long grieving should last. There is no sense of time in the loss of your child or loved one.

In the first year after Bryant's death, the term, "Time will heal," would not help me at all, it would only make me angry. I didn't un- der- stand why anyone would think that time would heal that kind of wound.

I also battled with a lot of anger towards people for not under- standing what I was feeling. I felt anger towards EMS for not saving my son, anger at the neighbor who lived across the street from where Bryant's accident took place because he didn't do enough to save my son, and even anger at Bryant for not wearing his seatbelt, even though I am still not convinced to this day that was true. I didn't have anger towards God, but I often wondered why God would take my son. I still have no answer to that question. I do believe now that time makes the wound easier to live with, but the wound never heals; it never goes away. Living with your own pain and the feelings of loss and helplessness is only one factor in the equation of this difficult tragedy. I cannot stress enough how important it is to remember that your entire family has been affected; they've experienced pain and loss, too, and must come to terms with their own deep hurt. As a mother of a child you want to protect your children from pain. One of the most difficult issues for me came in having to witness the re- action of Bryant's death and how it impacted my whole family and my close friends. We were living in Louisiana, my parents were in

Arkansas and there we all were in Tennessee where we had family and friends from six different states coming together to love one another and say good-bye to Bryant. But soon after, everyone separates in a way. They each return to their own lives. Days, months and years go by and everyone has to grieve and heal in their own way. Some avoid dealing with it at all and live years in denial, which is al- most certain to come back and affect them negatively. I often tried to hide my true pain. I didn't want anyone to see how bad off I really was at times in fear they would have me committed for therapy. Much of the time, I pretended I was all right in some way but in truth it was a façade and I was depressed. I still have my moments. I have moved past the self-pity of being the mom who lost her child.

I have too much healthy pride by nature to stay in a place of misery for too long. I didn't want my family or close friends to know the haunting and isolation I felt inside. I have always been a determined woman which I will agree can be labeled as "hardheaded" or even "control freak," and there have been times in my life upon reflection where I honestly felt I had accomplished and endured where others would have likely given up, but this was so different. My emotional state sunk lower than I ever thought it would go. I had no clear direction where I was going from wherever I was -- for myself or for others who depended on me. At one time or another we will all be faced with the dark journey of grief. While nearly everyone has experienced the loss of a loved one at one time or another, losing a child is probably the most difficult loss of all.

The best thing you can do in this type of situation is keeping your remarks simple and genuine. We need someone there for us to hold our hand, uplift us and console us. There are sensitive and insensitive ways to offer help, but don't judge someone too harshly that has never walked a mile in your shoes. I had and continue to have countless gestures from those just wanting to help. Letting someone in and allow them to see your broken heart is not easy for some, especially if you are supposed to be the strong one in the family and also with your group of friends. Accepting kindness from someone can also help them heal and get through their own hurts and struggles, so don't deny someone their offer of love on their journey to peace. Losing Bryant from this life has changed my life forever, as it will yours if you are ever faced with such. Today, I can feel deeper and much more intense than I have ever before in my life. I can't believe how some people perceive and deal with the problems they encounter when they are in reality so fixable and mine, on the other hand, is so permanent. Once I began writing in a journal off and on four months after Bryant died, it wasn't long before I began to think about writing a book. Every mother puts their child on a pedestal, and I not only wanted to write about Bryant and how we keep his memory alive, I wanted to hopefully reach a lost soul crying out for anything to give them comfort as I had been given in the face of heart-wrenching and mind numbing loss. I want to make it clear, however, that the act of accomplishing this was never easy to do. Finding time to write, keeping my notes for years and allowing myself to go back in time face the feelings of hopelessness were always tantamount to a form of self-torture in some ways. But, I found over time that writing gave me a way out of the dark hole of sadness and served instead to give me a rediscovered voice with a richer tone.

I talked about Bryant and the feelings of loss to individuals sometimes who didn't know me that well simply because the conversation was started. There is a good reason why it's taken me so long to write this book and that's because God wasn't done with me, He was and still is taking me on my journey in order to reach people that need to hear my story. "He comforts us in all our troubles so that we can comfort others. When they are troubled, we will be able to give them the same comfort God has given us." 2 Corinthians 1:4 my story has reached and impacted some people for different reasons and it continues to give me peace to talk about Bryant and my "new normal." I hope and pray without ceasing that my words do, in fact, bring comfort to a mother who has lost a child or to anyone who has suffered the loss of a close relationship. I have had to adjust and accept life as it is now. I still can't drive upon an accident without feeling a profound emptiness in the pit of my gut. I immediately pray for their soul and then I pray for their mother. I feel a connection with a mother who has been through what I have been through, and although I have buried my grandparents and I miss them so much, I believe the loss of your child is the worst loss you can endure.

Your child is gone and you are helpless, there is nothing you can ever do to completely recover from it. It totally disrupts any normalcy you once knew. I have learned so much from my experience and I am eager to use it to the most benefit for others. I know some things in life we take for granted every day can be permanently removed suddenly without warning. My son spent 17 years on this earth. Although he didn't get to stay long, I see clearly how God used him in ways I don't even know about yet, and may never know. My own purpose is not fulfilled or I wouldn't still be alive. God isn't finished with my purpose in this life, and if you're reading my book he is not finished with you. We all have a purpose in life and God uses each of us to benefit one another. I am going to use this time to glorify God and reveal how God is good in all things.

CHAPTER 20

✴

My Child Lives:
Stories of Strength

ryant as a person on this Earth and how he lived affected so many people. The stories are endless about how a miracle here or one there has happened that could only come from Bryant or how Bryant's life somehow made them who they are today, or how, in his death, someone was saved. I asked Bryant's friends to share stories about Bryant from before and after his death to help me somehow illustrate this truth so you, too, can relate to how your child not only brought so much happiness to others but also how his or her life, that living soul, also continues to affect others even after they're gone from this physical presence. The first letter here was one I received from an anonymous acquaintance of Bryant's from several years before the accident. The rest, as you will see, are thoughts from close friends.

I met your son in 6th or 7th grade. Although he and I were not great friends, we had a lot of mutual friends. Carson, Taylor, Hannah, Brad, Alec, Myles etc. When I was in 8th grade I started having problems with my friends. I did not want to deal with it and definitely did not want to go to school. Your son once told me "You know man, I have NO idea what you're going through, but stop letting these people get to you and just be yourself. Who cares what they think." I have lived in Chicago for about a year now and go to college up here. Because of my lack of communication with my old friends today was the first I heard of what happened. It hit me like a ton of bricks. I had hardly been in contact with him at all since 8th grade and don't even remember the last time I saw him. My point is, there was a time in my life where I came very close to committing suicide between personal issues and family issues. It was people like your son that said things like he did that day that kept me from doing it. I am a very happy now and very fortunate to have had a friend or two like your son.

Regardless if he knew it or not, your son changed my life. And now to see what has happened, it has gotten me thinking even more about it. It is very sad to hear what has happened to such a good person. They say everyone is put on this earth for a reason. If I know anything about Bryant it is that a lot of people loved him and if he could change someone's life that he barely knew or spent time with, I can only imagine how many lives he has touched. I wish I would have heard about this sooner. I would have liked to be there for the funeral. Your son was an amazing person and I didn't even know him that well. The way he lived his life changed me, and now the way he has passed has changed me. I hope this doesn't upset you at all I only wanted to state how truly amazing you did at raising him and that if there is anything you need to let me know.

— Anonymous writer

Not a day goes by that I don't think about Bryant. At the young age of 17, he was a man amongst boys. People often ask me what was he like, and I can only reply by simply saying, "He was the best." In whatever I was doing, Bryant was right there with care and encouragement. Others have recognized his impact on me, and as a gift, a friend who didn't even know Bryant, gave me a necklace with his old baseball number.

Over the years, I've gained knowledge, made new friends, and engaged in new experiences. I've met some incredible people, people who have made me a better individual, but none quite like him. He made people feel valued with his love and support. I admired him to an endless degree. Bryant was my best friend, as he was too many.

When he passed, I was struck with a pain unimaginable, and a hole was left in my heart. I never felt so alone. However, as I've grown, so has my relationship with our Lord. Through genuinely loving others, Bryant completed God's will for him, and his time here was concluded.

Over time, that hole I felt began to fill, not merely scar. I felt Bryant's presence. I didn't simply move on from Bryant's death, but grew stronger, feeling a piece of him living inside me. Bryant always challenged me to become a better person, and because of him, I feel that continuous desire to improve. I miss my friend, but find comfort in knowing he's in a better place and has positively impacted as many people through his departure as he did when he was here. I look forward to the day when I can properly thank him. Bryant was truly the best.

— Cameron Baker

There isn't one specific action or event that fully portrays what made Bryant Kite special.

Although he was just a teenager and the youngest of our grade, he seemed to have an understanding of the world that was beyond his years. Bryant refused to get caught up in the hustle and bustle of everyday life. He realized the importance of not taking anything for granted, and lived as if each day was truly a gift. One example of this was on Bryant's last night with us.

He came to pick me up from home on our way out for the night. I saw his truck, and me always being in a hurry, quickly yelled bye to my parents and rushed out the door to meet him. However, Bryant was already out of his truck and walking up the driveway so that he could come inside to say hello to my folks.

I told him it wasn't a big deal and we should just head out. But Bryant would have nothing of it. Bryant never missed a chance to speak to others, and it often brightened their day. He was never in a rush, and saying hello to other people was more important to him than our plans.

This opportunity to see my parents one last time was seemingly so small, yet will never be replaced. I can think back now, though, and learn from Bryant to slow down, to appreciate time, and to "be easy" as he always was.

I, like many others, try to live each day like his last, with no chance of regrets.

— Brad Andrews

On the night that Bryant passed, I was in the midst of yet another petty fight with my high school girlfriend. Myles told me to come over and play Ping Pong, and because I wanted to end the shouting match I was having over the phone, I decided to make the short walk over to the McGuire's. I knew I would be late but figured there would still be a few stragglers hanging out in the garage. As I walked down the driveway, I was lucky enough to run into Bryant as he was walking up to his truck.

I don't even remember much of what was said, but I do remember instantly being in a better mood as we talked. He had that effect on people. It is a rare quality to be able to walk into a room; smile, and genuinely uplift others with your presence. Bryant could do that like no one else I have ever known. That night we only spoke for a minute, but I will always remember the last thing he said to me before he got into his truck:

"It was good to see you for this brief moment."

It certainly was – not only for that moment in the driveway that I will forever carry with me -- but also for the brief time in my life I was able to share with Bryant.

— Russell Powers

I will never forget the last play I completed with Bryant. Countless times since his death, I have envisioned that double-play ball leaving my hand and sailing to Bryant's first baseman's mitt.

As we jogged off the field after that, the last game of that summer, we were winners. Bryant was always a winner. While we made plenty of great memories on the field together, Bryant's presence in the classroom always made those typical dreaded school days better. He was entertaining and unafraid, a decent person that accepted me as a worthy classmate, teammate, and friend.

While we spent three years of high school together, experiencing some of the highs and lows of what high school had to offer, there were many others that knew him better and were closer to him than I. However, Bryant still had a special friendship with me.

That is how Bryant lived. He always had a special relationship with each of those around him.

—Ben Brewer

Bryant Kite (A poem)

As she picked up the phone, "He's gone" was all she heard as tears started streaming down her face. The one boy who had stolen her heart had moved far away and left her astray. She questions why God gave her such a special gift, only to take it away. The only answer from above is God wanted to teach this girl how to love. She'll never understand why God blessed her to share his last birthday, his last game, his last day, and his last kiss. Every memory leaving her with so many things to miss. The way he would kiss her cheek and rub her back, to the way he could braid her hair and give her that adorable stare. He had a gorgeous smile that could brighten her day, followed by all his "Be Easy" ways.

An indescribable feeling consumes her, as she is overwhelmed with love and support from family, friends, and strangers. From heartfelt hugs and letters to numerous messages and phone calls. Every single one reaching out to show they care and recognizing the feelings this boy and this girl shared. A thank you would be in- sufficient as every single thing helped this girl during her suffering. Suffering that extended far beyond this girl, but deeper to a mother who lost her pride and joy, and to a father who lost his only little boy. To a sister whose little brother is gone, with whom she shares an unbreakable bond. To a little brother who has to grow up without his hero, and to a best friend whose fights together were zero? And to a devastated team left to carry on while their stud first baseman is gone.

Looking out at that diamond, all she could think of was the crack from the last time that ball was hit by his bat. As he rounded third, his name in the roar of the crowd was all that was heard. A name that should no doubt be under "Most Attractive" when the annual comes out. A name that has impacted more lives than he could ever visualize.

Because of him, this girl's biggest fear has been erased as she can't wait for that day when she will see his face. The day when she can run into his arms at Heaven's gates and their tummies can reunite to communicate. Though their time together was short, they had a connection that showed whenever their big brown eyes glowed.

Forever in everyone's heart is where this boy will stay because he touched so many in such a special way.

—Taylor Rudolph 8/7/2007

I never wanted to think my son's death could bring a positive light to anyone or anything because in life he was so much more, and I wanted him, for him, to be so much more to others. But after God opened my heart, and I discovered I was truly listening to others, I have a new outlook on his death

Yes, it's hard, and, yes, I want him back every day, but I have to live with my 'new normal life' and that life is not dwelling on his death but celebrating his life, and celebrating who Bryant was and is – who Bryant is -- within others.

I can honestly say my son's graduating class is the most unified, intelligent, and warm and caring kids I have ever known. There were a large group of friends who pulled it all together and formed what we call today the Bryant Kite Scholarship Foundation.

The mission of the Bryant Kite Memorial Foundation is to give strength and courage to those affected by a loss of a loved one; to keep his spirit strong and ever present; to educate teenagers on safety awareness; and to provide scholarship support to students who best exemplify the outstanding qualities exhibited by Bryant during his time on Earth.

His close friends and family created the Bryant Kite Memorial Foundation. The inspiration for this endeavor evolved during numerous discussions by so many that loved   Bryant.

Bryant Kite Scholarship Foundation

Discussions and reflection on the intent of this memorial foundation settled on a simple yet substantial goal: to honor the memory of a fallen friend by educating and lifting other individuals to the heights of his or her personal best. The promise of this memorial foundation is one of encouragement, education and financial support. The scholarship recipient would be defined as an individual striving for harmony, academic distinction and athletic excellence. It's been six-and-a-half years since my son Bryant died in his horrible truck accident and the love for Bryant by not only is family but his friend's lives on. Members of the Cordova High School class of 2008 have all moved on from high school but Bryant stays with them forever. Some have graduated from college, married, and had children of their own and hold steady jobs. There are two young men, Cory and Brad, who continue to organize the BK5K, which is the annual 5K event we put on to raise funds for Bryant's scholarship. Cory and Brad, along with many friends and supporters, organize the BK5K each year in Memphis, TN. God will use every situation and every person you meet to add value or help you grow. All of us should go through life being a blessing to one another in some way.

It is those with giving hearts and sponsoring that allow us to be a blessing to others. We gave scholarship money each year to a deserving senior going to college. My son could have gone anywhere to college with his grades and athletic talent so it makes sense to provide someone else the same opportunity in Bryant's name. Every year we looked forward to being reunited with friends and families to celebrate Bryant's life not mourn his death. This year will be out last year as we draw the Foundation to a close after 10 years.

CHAPTER 21

✳

Above all know this

I recently heard a story about a young man that was a few years younger than Bryant but who played baseball with him in high school. This particular boy was one of those who looked up to Bryant, and after Bryant's death he carried a picture of him in his wallet. One-day traveling down the interstate, he was involved in an auto accident and his automobile caught fire. Everything had burned in- side his vehicle along with his wallet. In the wallet, chard and melted, he saw Bryant's picture. The only item to survive the crash was this picture of Bryant. He said he knew at that moment Bryant had helped save him from that accident and that the surviving picture was Bryant's way of letting him know he was protected.

When I am in a dark place, and believe me that place will come and go depending on the day, I can feel comfortable by seeing a red-bird or the #35. I truly believe my son is with the Lord but I also believe the Holy Spirit send signs of comfort for us. I told my family and friends about my red bird and of they smile with love. It wasn't until my friend Angela witnessed the comfort I felt when a red bird showed up at the exact moment I needed it, that someone – for the first time – really, truly understood. I have and can tell you about countless stories about my red bird. My most favorite story is the time I was privileged to be invited to a professional baseball game while working in California with co-workers. We had tickets right behind 3rd base about four rows up, and you felt like you were sitting on the field. I was feeling overwhelmed with the presence of Bryant for some reason. He loved baseball and I had never had the opportunity to bring him to a professional game although we had discussed it many times. This game was the Giants vs -- you guessed it – the Cardinals. There they were with their red birds on the front of their uniforms and right when I began to feel an overpowering urge to bust out in tears I heard the announcer say, "Next up, straight from the minors, making his debut is #35." I don't remember his name; only the instant contentment in knowing that was Bryant's spirit letting me know he was here with me. My favorite #35 story is the time we lived on the river and we had a dock in our backyard. During spring and summer months you could sit and watch the boats go by for hours.

This was Christmas time and it was very cold out- side. I couldn't shake the funk I was in so I walked outside and just sat on the dock. Within a few minutes of a heavy heart I heard a speedboat coming down the river. I hadn't heard a boat in months, it just wasn't the season to normally hear or see a boat on the water. As the speedboat moved directly in front of me, I noticed it was white boat with a huge number 35 on its side. Nothing else on the boat except this number. I couldn't believe it at first, then I just looked up and said out loud, "I feel your son and I will stop feeling sorry for myself today." You may see a pet do something that makes you believe or feel tranquility just by holding something that belonged to child. I once heard about a mother who lost a child that had a bird peck on her window every time she cried and only when she cried. Today my red bird is still active. This year for Christmas my daughter bought us both red bird ornaments for our Christmas trees. Bryant's friends, and even my friends and their kids, display Bryant's number 35 on game jerseys and at other events. My daughter Kristina and I have a wonderful relationship and we decided one day to make candles in Bryant's honor. With the help of one of Bryant and Kristina's longtime friends, Lindsey, who is a graphic designer today, we developed a trade- marked logo for our candle and became Like Mother-Like Daughter.

Even though we only sell our candles to friends and a few local stores, we have more joy just making them for fun as gifts to others. It's okay to have feelings of loss but it's not okay to stay in that dark place of sadness. Keeping a memory alive and yet not living your life is not okay. There are various ways to cope with sadness and depression but it's not okay to just say, "I want to be sad." Don't mistake guilt as a way of proving you were a good mother. You are still alive here on Earth and God has a plan for you just as he did, and still does, for your child or loved one. Believe God! Believe in God; but most important of all, know God! This is what my precious baby boy taught me in life, in his death, and through his life everlasting. I knew the first moment I laid eyes on Bryant that he was a gift from God– a gift that would last a lifetime. Praise God!

John 14:1-4

"Let not your hearts be troubled. Believe in God; believe also in me. In my Father's house are many rooms. If it were not so, would I have told you that I go to pre- pare a place for you? And if I go and prepare a place for you, I will come again and will take you to myself, that where I am you may be also. And you know the way to where I am going."

Romans 8:16-17
"The Spirit himself bears witness with our spirit that we are
children of God, and if children, then heirs -- heirs of God and fel-
low heirs with Christ, provided we suffer with him in order that we
may also be glorified with him"

2 Corinthians 5:6-8

"So we are always of good courage. We know that while we are at home in the body we are away from the Lord, for we walk by faith, not by sight. Yes, we are of good courage, and we would rather be away from the body and at home with the Lord"

Psalm 23:4

"Even though I walk through the valley of the shadow of death, I will fear no evil"

Psalm 116:15

"Precious in the sight of the LORD is the death of his saints."

John 10:27-29

"My sheep hear my voice, and I know them, and they follow me. I give them eternal life, and they will never perish, and no one will snatch them out of my hand. My Father, who has given them to me, is greater than all, and no one is able to snatch them out of the Father's hand." (Jesus speaking)

Revelation 14:13

"And I heard a voice from heaven saying, "Write this: Blessed are the dead who die in the Lord from now on." "Blessed in-deed," says the Spirit, "that they may rest from their labors, for their deeds follow them!"

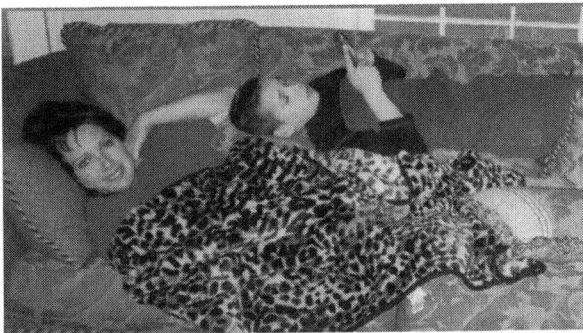

Live to know God; know God to live! Forever. – AMEN

For more information on:
Step into Your Purpose & Free Resources
Visit www.cherierickard.com

Social Media Contact Cherie Rickard
Author Facebook Fan Page:
www.facebook.com/authorcherierickard
Instagram: @iamcherierickard
Twitter: @cherierickard

Author's Note

In the beginning, I wrote....

I did so not realizing my journal notes would evolve into this book. When I made the decision to actually write my book, I had no idea how others would respond or receive my writings. I just simply knew I needed to write for me, for my family, for healing, for therapy, and also so my experience and my suffering may somehow benefit and comfort someone else. I reached for anything to gain comfort in my grief. I know for me, just reading about someone else that understood my pain and sorrow gave me some type of relief -- I am not the only person on earth that suffers from tragic loss, from a life that is forever changed. Since July 12, 2007, I rarely look back on descriptive details of that first wake-up call at 2 in the morning except to write. I will always be able to recount the days when I felt complete despair from the loss of my son. I knew God, but I didn't begin to fathom what I was going through. There was no light, not one that I could see. I prayed to God that my son continues to live on, to matter to others for as long as I live, and longer.

For the rest of my life I vowed to myself to set a daily goal to try to make each day the best possible and to devote myself to being the best I can be for myself and for others. I asked myself many times before my son died if I had a purpose. Is your purpose clear? I asked God to show me my purpose, and although all of the details that comprise my purpose have not yet been revealed or fulfilled, I know in my heart this book is one of them. I will fail from time to time, but I will continue to fight and pick myself up for the love and grace of God's purpose in my life. God showed me this – through Bryant; he used Bryant to teach me things about Him. The lessons continue.

The light I now see is bright.

Although I had made the decision to write a book, I still had no idea, no practical under- standing, of how I would actually do that. I just wrote and waited on God's timing, and then one day he made it very clear how that would happen. Todd Horne and I grew up walking to elementary school together and were friends all during junior high and some high school. We parted ways when I had to leave all my friends at a crucial teenage time and attend a different high school because the school system decided to draw new boundaries. Remember, even when you think the worst thing has happened to you God can turn that around. More than 30 years later, Todd and I, by chance, reconnected and the rest of the story is written in this book. Todd, with many years of writing, editing and publishing skill, has taken on this project with passion and it has been a blessing to partner with you on this book. You and Ashley are greatly appreciated. I want to thank the Cordova High School class of 2008 for always remembering Bryant and making him such a large part of your senior year. Although he isn't here physically, Bryant is always with you spiritually. There are so many precious people who continue to recognize Bryant in many ways from still selecting #35 for game jerseys, to visiting his gravesite and by attending the 5K each year in Memphis.

Dedication

To all my faithful friends from Louisiana and Tennessee who stood by me on that miserable July day, and who still stand with me in support and friendship.

To Pam and Tracie who each gives so much of yourselves and would drop anything if I called -- my heart is full of love for you both.

Megan, my loving friend of 33 years who will also celebrate her birthday on the anniversary of Bryant's burial, I don't know what I would have done without you.

To Angela, who God placed directly in my path only four months after that tragic day, I am blessed and thankful for every day we have had together in laughter and tears. Thank you for all the encouragement in writing my book.

To my parents, Larry & Glenna Rowland, my sister Carla and my nephew Holden, thank you for allowing me to cry and lean on your shoulder even when you wanted to cry yourself. Thank you to my brother Larry, who always believed in my red bird, and for making one for me to carry every day.

My family is the glue to healing. Deep gratitude goes to Cory and Brad who organize the BK5K, the committee of volunteers, and to the Board of Directors that help make the Bryant Kite scholarship possible. All of your sacrifices to keep the event and scholarship going are so greatly appreciated. Heartfelt thanks to the Kite Family and Rickard Family, who love me and who stood with me. Sincere thoughtfulness and love to my sweet beautiful children Kristina and Carson, who have had to endure so much and yet continue to make me so proud every day of my life. To my stepdaughter Mackenzie, who has always loved me even in my darkest hour.

Profound recognition to my husband Wendell, who is MY ROCK and who carried my heart through the funeral and the years after. The love you gave Kristina and Bryant can only be rewarded in heaven. You are the best father and husband I could ever hope to ask for. God blessed me with you!

ABOUT THE AUTHOR

"Life is a journey that each of us are blessed with at birth. We all will encounter pleasure and pain but what makes us unique is how we transform our pain into power. In 2007 my life would take a turn no mother can even imagine unless you've walked in my shoes. My beautiful 17-year-old son Bryant died tragically in an auto accident coming home one night trying to make curfew. For 7 years I used a pen and paper and later my laptop to write down every pain, struggle and milestone I encountered after the worst day of my life. Facing a cross road in life with depression and destruction versus using my pain and regaining power I chose to live in a way that would honor my son's memory and give glory to God.

I would have never imagined I would become an International Published Author/Speaker/Grief and Empowerment Strategist writing and delivering a powerful message on Building Confidence, overcoming tragedy, grief recovery, making your mess your message and learning to live a life with passion and purpose. It is a message I learned from my own life and one that I use to help others apply to their own lives". - *Cherie*

Cherie's award-winning book, ***Wake-Up Call...A Mother's Grief Journey***, is a true story written after her 17-year-old son that was killed tragically in an auto accident. Cherie's widely recognized 2nd book, ***Healing Your Wounded Spirit*** hit #1 on Amazon in Love & Loss and gives guidance and support others need after divorce, death of a loved-one and broken friendships. She delivers a stimulating message based on her 3rd book ***Strong Women*** which will not only guide you but show you how to improve your life through boosted confidence, interviewing skills, self-esteem and independence. Cherie's new book, ***How to Live a Life with Passion & Purpose*** will not only push you into action but show you how to take action in life to get what you want and deserve.

Cherie frequently appears as a featured guest and expert on numerous Broadcast & Podcast radio programs and is a speaker & mentor. Cherie has been featured in Publishers Weekly, awarded special recognition through several Book Awards and has had numerous articles published on other websites and social media. She is a motivational speaker to a wide variety of audiences; including business and networking organizations, social and charitable organizations, students (ranging from high school to college), women's organizations, business development, self-publishing and authors as well as the healthcare, hospice and bereavement industries.

Cherie's skills and experience expands with over 20 years in the Healthcare industry as a Registered Nurse, Medical Professional, Business development, marketing specialist, Grief & Empowerment Strategist. She is a member of the Women Speakers Association and E-women Network.

Her powerful and passionate message educates, inspires, motivates, teaches and offers practical guidance to those who have experienced any kind of tragedy, set back or challenge in their lives.

Made in the USA
Columbia, SC
06 November 2017